Best of luck

Ben Grant

Balletsa Inc

All inquiries should be forwarded to the publisher at info@michelepaiva.com of Balletsa Inc.

ISBN: 978-09832915-2-7

Published: January 2011

First Edition

Bernie Parent with Michele Paiva & Dean Smith

JOURNEY THROUGH RISK AND FEAR

Bernie Parent

Co-Authored & Produced with

Michele Paiva & Dean Smith

Balletsa Inc Publishing

<u>*Credits*</u>

Author: Bernie Parent

Co-Author, Publisher: Michele Paiva

Co-Author, Manager: Dean Smith

Editor: Michelle Andrews

Daniel Morroni: Morroni Custom Clothing

Cover Photo Credits: Eric Bennett

Bernie Parent with Michele Paiva & Dean Smith

Dedications

(Paiva) With thanks to G_d, to friends and family, my children Alexandria and Nicholas; may this book be a reference for years to come. I want to thank the enterprising and generous Dean Smith, for seeing the spark and laying the path for my own journey. To Bernie, words can't describe what you have come to mean to me, perhaps best described with a smile and your, "eh!" does it best!

(Smith) I want to thank the people at the end of the day that I rely on for love and support, for the people who have sacrificed the most in my journey's and allowed me to face risk and fear in my endeavors. With love, to Caroline, my incredible wife; and to my children, Tommy, Katie and Amy you are my world. It goes without saying to thank Bernie, who has defined the meaning of a true friend, and taught me how to become a better quality human being. Frenchie thanks for coming into my life

(Parent) I want to thank Carol, and my children, Chuck, Bernie and Kim, and my grandchildren Sam, Katie, Maddy, Tina, Jake and Bernie III. To Ed Snider, words cannot describe the gratitude that I have for you. For taking the risk on a young goalie and facing the fear of the unknown and bringing hockey to the great city of Philadelphia- thank you for all you have done, and to my friends, family and fans, for being a part of my pack, and allowing me to be a part of your pack as well.

Bernie Parent with Michele Paiva & Dean Smith

February 24th, 1975, there was a famous photo

that graced the cover of Time Magazine, titled,

"War on Ice", with Parent behind his mask, his

eyes penetrating. February 17, 1979,

those eyes would be blinded.

Now, sight-restored both physically

and with vision, the mask is off,

with even more passion and intensity.

This book is dedicated to everyone beginning the journey through risk and fear.

Bernie Parent with Michele Paiva & Dean Smith

The Journey

Bernie Parent with Michele Paiva & Dean Smith

Preface

A dog is well cared for, with food and a roof over his head. He doesn't have to want for much, as it is provided. He looks outside all the time, enjoying the view from the window, and every now and then, even gets to go for a walk. He is content enough but he always is looking outside, and is always interested in what is happening just beyond his reach, outside the door. Though he feels quite content, he is not fulfilled. It's not natural for him to be held captive. When you think of a dog, you may get an image of the animal sitting at the foot of someone, or curled up waiting for life to begin, or awaiting patiently (at least on the external) the next treat to be given to him In short, a very trained, controlled animal.

Now, take the wolf. The wolf hunts for his food. He struggles a little more, and he doesn't have a roof over his head unless he finds his own shelter. No one is looking out for the wolf. But the wolf is beyond content. He is fulfilled. He knows how to survive and he knows how to make the best of each situation. He isn't held captive. In fact, he is free. He really has everything the dog has - with the addition of freedom. When you imagine the wolf, you probably imagine him standing, looking either into your eyes or out into the distance, with strength and mystery. He controls his own destiny, and takes a treat when he decides, not when someone else decides. He is free.

The wolf knows how to live with *risk*, and knows how to push through *fear*. He knows how to cope, how to plan, how to reach goals and even to dream, with

Bernie Parent with Michele Paiva & Dean Smith

passion, his desires. The wolf, *not* the captive dog, is fulfilled with life, not just content, because the wolf carves his own life, not melds to someone else's image of what he should be. Are you sitting in your home, class or office right now and feeling more like a dog or a wolf? Are you "just" content or are you very satisfied? Do you look at risk as a part of life or avoid it? Do you avoid fear or look it in the eye and embrace its opportunity? Do you make your own decisions or do you mold yourself to make others happy only? Are you looking outside of your window with the world passing by or are you standing with strength and living each moment with zeal.

My name is Bernie Parent, and you probably know me as an NHL Hall of Fame inductee for my work as a goaltender for the Philadelphia Flyers as well as a professional hockey player in Canada and in the United States. Perhaps you may know me as one of the "Broad Street Bullies", or as a twice-Stanley Cup winner with my teammates. Although integral to my success and life, this part of my life is just one small facet of who I am and I have a message for you. Taking my life trials and tribulations, and the lessons I've had to learn, some the hard way, I am able to guide you to find the *wolf within yourself*, to push *past* risk and fear, to not be captive by your own fears and anxieties, and to become the self-sufficient, satisfied, passionate and empowered person that you are within.

There is a reason that they say it is a "dog-eat-dog" world; because unhappy people focus on unhappy tasks. People afraid of risk never seek higher places and in low places people hurt one another and themselves.

Bernie Parent with Michele Paiva & Dean Smith

This is not the way we should live. In my darkest hours, literally, my life changed dramatically. I thought that I was a wolf because of some of the risks I took earlier in life, and fears I pushed through; until I realized I had been captive by my own boundaries. In those hours, when I laid in darkness for days on end, in a hospital room, my entire being was changed. Though, at the time, I thought I was becoming weaker, I was simply a captive dog transforming itself into a free wolf.

It is my goal to help shed light into your own darkness and bring your inner light to the surface so that you can be free from your own captivity. Before I give you a bit of how I came into the sport of hockey, let me start at my transformation in my hospital bed; the turning point that ended my career in as a hockey player, but began my life of freedom from captivity. The world was dark and I could not see. The only place I could focus was inward.

Bernie Parent with Michele Paiva & Dean Smith

Bernie Parent with Michele Paiva & Dean Smith

Introduction

It was a day not unlike most other days. Nothing
extraordinary about the day at all really, and if you are
like me, you tend to take for granted days that are
somewhat uneventful without realizing it. Of course,
you don't really take them for granted but you don't
give them much thought.

I did the ritual on game days; I didn't intend on having
a ritual it just sort of happened that way. I woke up at
about 7 a.m., read the newspaper and had a cereal
breakfast with the kids before they went to school.
Then, at about 9 that morning, as was typical, I went to
the rink. I got the sticks ready. We had about four or
five sticks normally and though they all looked the
same, they had different feels, so you had to get them
all ready depending upon what you wanted to use. We
did the work ourselves on them, so we spent time taking
the old tape off and putting new tape on them. Like we
always did, we put our equipment on. So, I put my
equipment on and skated around for a while and got hot
and sweaty; then showered and headed home. All of
this was typical. I ate a late lunch, and as usual on game
days I had sirloin steak, with ten mushrooms. Don't ask
me why ten mushrooms, it just ended up to be a ritual.
Then, showered and full, I took a nap in bed with
Tinkerbell, my German shepherd. After my nap, I'd
watch the Three Stooges. I always felt being happy was

Bernie Parent with Michele Paiva & Dean Smith

the best thing for anyone; as when you are happy good things happen to you. I didn't know that at the time though; I learned it much later. However, at the time, I just knew watching the Three Stooges made me laugh and so that is what I did. After watching, I got ready, like I always did, and was at the rink by five. The only thing on my mind was the game against the New York Rangers that I had to get ready for, but remember, that was my job. Like you, I just got up in the morning,

I ate breakfast and did my thing like any other day as I outlined previously. I was basking in the light of life; everything I had set out to do was happening. My childhood dream had come true. I was playing professional ice hockey. I took a bit of this for granted perhaps. So, it was time to get to work; I put the pads on, the protective mask, nothing was different. Little did I know such an uneventful day would change so quickly. In a few hours, a moment would arrive which would change my life forever. On the afternoon of February 17th, 1979, Defenseman, Jimmy Watson was on the ice trying to move the Rangers' Don Maloney from in front of the net and they collided. In an effort to watch the puck, I turned to view it going from the left to the right, and, at that moment, the one vulnerable area on my mask was exactly the spot where Watson's errant blade caught. I felt intense pain and pressure, and everything went dark.

Bernie Parent with Michele Paiva & Dean Smith

Watson accidentally put the blade of his stick into the right eye slit of the mask. I was a little disoriented and in pain and my instinct was to just push the mask off of my face. I heard the crowd and surrounding sounds, and just felt like I needed to get off the ice, immediately. I knew it was bad. I don't even know how I managed to skate off the ice as well as I did. I've looked at tapes of it and can see that I just looked in shock and in pain.

My right eye had been pushed back into the socket and had irreversible damage. The damage to my eye was physical, and though I had hoped to return to the game, I had a lot more going through my mind. In what seemed like both an eternity and seconds, the Flyers trainers and doctors were surrounding me, taking great care, and before I knew it, I was off the ice, out of the Spectrum and taken to Wills Eye Hospital in Philadelphia. There was a lot of blood pouring out of the eye and doctors tried to stabilize it. The eye that had escaped the blade also suffered injury, and I was in complete darkness. I know I'm repeating myself but the darkness was encompassing not only my vision, but also my very being. At the hospital, surrounded by darkness, I lay in the bed and, quite frankly, was scared. I lived in darkness now, not basking in the light of a passionate career. Darkness. It's something that enters everyone's life at one time or another, whether they invite it in or not. Sometimes in the greatest moments of despair, there is darkness. I had darkness before this,

Bernie Parent with Michele Paiva & Dean Smith

and I'll talk about that later, but nothing to this degree
of despair; these moments were the darkest of my life.
One moment I was living my dream, the next moment,
a nightmare. Lying in a hospital bed for just over two
weeks, while doctors worked on eye tissue, I waited,
and waited more, only to have them go back to work
again in the eye tissue. It was bleak, dark and terrifying.
A lot of times during those days, I would ask when my
vision was going to come back and the answer I always
got was that they were not sure if it would, and if it did,
to what ability I'd be able to see if at all. I wondered
what it would be like not to ever see my family again. I
wondered what it would be like to not see my children
grow up and change as they matured, to not be able to
look into my wife's eyes again, and to not even be able
to see my own reflection as I aged. These thoughts
haunted me while I was awake, sitting alone in my
hospital room, propped in the bed, learning to balance
myself in the encompassed blackness that was now my
reality and life. In the night, the sweat from nightmares
oozed from every pore as I woke, freezing and
shivering, to the realization that I could not even put a
light on, to see, but had to wake with the same darkness
in which the nightmares flourished. Then, something
changed. It was almost a month to the day that I became
blind, and my vision was slowly returning. However, as
the doctors walked toward me with downcast faces,
their mood clearly uncomfortable, I knew that

Bernie Parent with Michele Paiva & Dean Smith

something was very wrong. "Your eyesight is coming
back of course, and we are happy, but what we do
know, is that it won't come back nearly enough for you
to continue your career. Your career as a professional
hockey player is over. We are sorry," they said. Tears
filled my eyes, as my nightmare simply changed paths. I
had so many questions about my future. At the time, my
source of income was as a hockey player and I had a
life I was used to, as many of you are used to your own
lives. You don't want to change, you want things to get
better or at least stay the same, not get worse. I was the
same as you; I didn't want my life to take a turn for the
worse yet again. I was thinking about the unknown and
trying to figure out how I'd sustain my family: a wife
and son and daughter. My short, sweet taste of hopes
and dreams from my sight returning had turned sour.
Here I was, not appreciating a gift of sight just days
after it finally was returning, only to realize the problem
wasn't physical but much deeper. Luckily, I had people
in my life that were there for me; it was then that I
realized it is impossible to succeed in life by yourself,
but just like in sports, just like in ice hockey, you need a
team to be successful. You do your part, you take
responsibility but you work with others for optimal
success. My team was there for me. The Philadelphia
Flyers helped me beyond the ice; they taught me how to
be successful in business, and they were like a compass
guiding me in the correct direction. They had become

Bernie Parent with Michele Paiva & Dean Smith

instrumental, even more than when I was on the ice,
they were much more important to me off the ice now.
But like I said, you have to be responsible for yourself. I
took courses and learned in any way I could, from
mentors and friends to taking business courses.
Although shy by nature, I learned how to survive in a
world where one needs to interact; because when my
career and identity as a hockey player ended so quickly,
I needed to remember the lessons I learned in those two
weeks laying in a hospital bed, in the darkness both
physically and emotionally, and allow myself to take a
risk; feel the fear and plow through both. I could have
vanished into the darkness. Maybe you have been in
that darkness and maybe you are there now. Perhaps
you are feeling that life simply isn't as illuminated as it
could; and you may be right. In fact, I bet you are
correct; because in all of the years leading up to my
injury, I thought I took risks, and plowed through fear;
even being labeled a "Broad Street Bully" wasn't what
true fearlessness was all about. Overcoming fear meant
digging into my resources and spirit and taking risks
that were out of my comfort zone. I went off the ice and
into that hospital bed a dog, but while there, while I
healed, I transformed into a wolf. As I said, we all need
a team. I'm going to be your coach and on your team, to
take you from dog to wolf on your own journey. It's
time to transform.

Bernie Parent with Michele Paiva & Dean Smith

Part One

Chapter 1

Finding Your Purpose

Everyone talks about purpose and living your purpose
for happiness and self-satisfaction, but no one easily
explains how one finds that purpose. I've talked to
many people who say that they want to have "purpose"
in their lives but don't quite know what purpose is, and
certainly most adults, much less young adults, haven't
figured out their purpose. It's why so many people are
in careers that they do not enjoy or are in relationships
from which they seek fulfillment yet gleaning almost no
satisfaction from. First let's really go backward a bit,
and understand what purpose is. Purpose is a result of a
goal or intention. In the best-case scenario, it is a true
reason for existence. It is a place in which you feel
fulfilled, happy and on top of the world. It is your inner
purpose, dormant, come alive. When I was in that
hospital bed, I started out saying "Why me?" Then, I
started focusing on "Why not me?" as I realized that
there was a greater power within me, driving me, and
that my existence or purpose was not solely ice hockey.
Professional ice hockey was a means to get to my
higher purpose. It was enjoyable, it was a part of who I
was, and who I am, and it shaped me, but it was not my

Bernie Parent with Michele Paiva & Dean Smith

sole purpose, nor my only intention in life. In that darkness I had time to reflect, and unlike you, I was forced to do nothing but reflect, and because of that gift, I urge you to take time to reflect as well. Make it a priority. I was born in 1945 on April 3rd, in Quebec, Canada, the youngest of seven children in my middle class family that struggled to make ends meet. Things were not easy as you can imagine. Though life wasn't easy and some things were a real struggle, we still had each other and, though cliché, it was true. As a kid, I could describe myself as a dreamer, as many children are, though with luck, dreams never left me. In some people, their dreams slowly fizzle and they forget their dreams, though I never did.

As a preteen, at about twelve years old, I really began to play and enjoy organized hockey. Although there were, or felt like, two hundred people telling me I couldn't play hockey and would never make it, I kept dreaming, and playing, in spite of the fact that I didn't have a natural ability or build for it. However, that didn't stop me, thanks to my dreams. That dreamer quality may have molded me a bit into the black sheep of the family, because I was the only one that didn't take the more intellectual route, instead focusing on a kinetic route through sports. Black sheep or not, my passion for hockey grew as did the support of my family. My father was quiet and a hard worker and my mother was the caregiver and was always at my games.

Bernie Parent with Michele Paiva & Dean Smith

The support from my mother was, I realized, increasingly important to me while growing up, as it was the foundation of the acceptance that I needed. I remember one time I was trying out for a team as a teenager and the rest of the kids were skating so quickly. We were being timed; their times were more like 15 seconds and mine was closer to 25 seconds. I wasn't impressive in terms of skill or speed at that time, however, the coach asked me to be a goalie. There are different skates for goalies even at that age and level, but my parents couldn't afford the correct skates as I recall; which didn't bother me really because, to me, skates were skates. I was not letting that be an obstacle. Well, it was horrible. The other team ended up making 21 goals against me; the coach was trying to tactfully dissuade me. Well, that was the end of that, or so I thought. Again, my family was supportive, though they didn't say much, my mother, especially, let me know that it was just a setback, and that life would go on. I took her advice and knew why the other team scored against me; I didn't have great balance on the ice, so I practiced every day on the still ice-covered streets. Then, the coach called. It seems that the other kid who had replaced me got hurt and they needed me. It was a milestone for me because I did it and it worked. I was up to par enough to go on, because I knew I had two choices only with that dream; to make it flourish or allow it to die. In the introduction, I spoke about

Bernie Parent with Michele Paiva & Dean Smith

teamwork, and just having a support system of family who were, at that time, part of my team and I didn't realize it. As a dreamer, I had people I looked up to, beyond my family that I respected very much. One such person was the Montreal Canadians goalie, Jacques Plante. His sister lived next door to my parents' home and I would wait and watch him from behind bushes in my parents' yard when he would visit his sister. I wanted to be just like him; and here he was so close to me. I remember he smoked cigars, and oddly I think it is why I smoked cigars as I got older; funny how what you want comes to you and can shape how you create your life. Later in life, I ended up being a teammate of his and, at the time, I thought I had it all, but I didn't realize it was just one of my passions Thus, with the imbalance that I felt, there wasn't a sense of true purpose as a whole person, especially when that one passion was taken away from me on February 17th in 1979. **To have purpose is to be a wolf.** Purpose means freedom to achieve, even if that is a rough road ahead of you; it is your choice. People stay in careers that they don't enjoy because they lost their purpose, because they opt to not take risks and live in the constraints of fear. All freedom comes with risk. People have been trained to not take a risk, and that risk is bad. Risk can be exciting; it is simply how you look at it. Risk is part of each dream, and a necessity for that dream to materialize. If you fear risk, that exciting

Bernie Parent with Michele Paiva & Dean Smith

moment that you can sacrifice one thing to gain something else, you won't take the risk. It is true, the larger the risk, the larger the reward. There is the possibility, though that you may sacrifice something and not get the reward, and that is what people fear. However, you could look at it this way; the more you risk, the more you are going to have an opportunity for a reward. Would you rather risk nothing and be unhappy for sure, or risk something and have a chance at being happy? Would you risk a lot to reap a bigger reward?

How much would you risk for your dream?

If you wouldn't risk anything, what fears are holding you back?

Bernie Parent with Michele Paiva & Dean Smith

Bernie Parent with Michele Paiva & Dean Smith

Chapter 2

Fear

Fears are circles of endless despair. Fears go against dreams and they go against purpose. If you are focused on your fear you can't possibly be focused on your purpose and you most certainly are not living toward fulfilling dreams. The difference between fear and a dream is that the thoughts of a dream help you to feel good, while the thoughts of fear help you to feel badly. Later we will talk about how you can control your journey and thoughts, but for now, let's take a little time to uncover fear. Not focus on fear, just to uncover it and showcase how it has very little power unless you let it. I had incredible fear when I was about 16 years old and I opted to leave my home country, without knowing the English language, to come to the States to play hockey for the Boston Bruins when they drafted me. These were all choices; all opportunities. I could have been afraid and not seized that opportunity or string of opportunities, but instead I used that fear and turned it into a positive energy. At the time though, I didn't know this, or shall I say, I wasn't aware of what I was naturally doing. I was simply following my heart and dream, and thus, on a path to my purpose. I still feel choked up when I think about it. Here I was leaving my

family at just 16 years old. I'd write to my brother Jack
weekly and share with him my frustrations and fears,
and, you know what, he was always supportive. That
was something that helped me through that fear. Later
on, even though I talk a lot about being a lone wolf, I
want you to realize every strong lone wolf really never
alone; they have a pack. They are den animals and, in
order to be successful in the wild, they need the power
of the pack. Jack, my brother, was just that: a part of my
pack. A pack isn't just family or friends, and it isn't just
someone you work with. A pack member is anyone who
is willing to help you. You are a part of many packs and
many individuals are a part of your pack. You don't
have to share common goals, just a willingness to help
each the other in any way that makes your lives easier
and more productive. We will talk later about
cultivating your pack. Fear can play a big part in lessons
you learn, because it can help you to be open to
learning. For some people, fear is in fact, a teacher who
is helping you with a life lesson.   For me, when I was a
kid, it was my family and their dedication, my early
team mates and coaches and as a teenager it was Bill
Long; my coach who guided me as I honed my craft at
the rink in Niagara Falls. He would talk about angles all
the time and yes, I was a late bloomer and maybe that is
why I just didn't get it with the "angles". I felt
frustrated and fearful, as if I should have known better.
I didn't really have much technical training, and now

Bernie Parent with Michele Paiva & Dean Smith

that I was in the professional ranks, I was scared
because I didn't know what my coach was talking
about. Well, for me, I didn't let fear stop me. I asked for
and took direction, and learned that it was about
blocking the puck, and getting the correct angle from
the place where the puck was heading; like physics on
ice. I practiced and learned and learned and practiced;
that is how I became an angle goalie. They don't teach
you purpose in schools, and they do institute fear: fear
of doing wrong, fear of annoying the teacher, fear of a
bad grade. I like many people, found school to be
boring. Let's be honest, many times one teacher may
inspire us but on the whole, schools are focused on
tedious details and the students are not enthralled
because they don't understand why they need to know
these topically meaningless details. I for one, felt
trapped by the tedious nature of school and it's
meaninglessness to my life at the time, because there
was no big picture attached to the details. However,
when I practiced hockey, the small details were very
important to me because I could see the big picture.
Now realize, some people thrive on the details and for
them, that *is* the big picture; we all work forward and
are going in the same direction, but if you are like me,
sometimes you need to understand the big picture more,
or have a sense of purpose in order for the details to
have meaning. I saw the details in practicing hockey as
freeing. I saw what I did not know or hadn't mastered

Bernie Parent with Michele Paiva & Dean Smith

as obstacles to overcome and I had a passion to get to those goals. I risked some lazy couch time to get out and sweat it out during practice. The risk was worth it. My fear of not being good enough was overshadowed by the reward that I may be good enough. You and I are very similar; for you and I, freedom comes with a bit of risk, always. For you and I, having the right people in our lives helps us to achieve great things. If we have the wrong people in our lives, we are simply putting up our own obstacles as well as the obstacles set in place by nature. We have to depend upon how we feel inside. We need to pay attention to our reactions, and we need to guide our feelings and reactions. We need to look at change and not be afraid of it, and we need to look at something that may be potentially destructive as an obstacle not a debilitation. We need to do what I figured out in that hospital bed and not say "why me?" but rather, "why not me!" I recently had lunch with a few friends and I said to them, "What is it that you love?" We talked about that for a while. Why? Because what you love is what your passion is. Focus on your passion or passions. You may have more than one. What your passions are, and what you overcome obstacles for, what you dream about; that is your purpose. Hockey was <u>on the way</u> to my purpose. It was <u>part</u> of the journey, and for a kid who didn't know the language, and was away from his family and feeling alone, who didn't feel that confident in his technical

Bernie Parent with Michele Paiva & Dean Smith

skills for the very sport he was professionally playing, *that* can be a scary place. I finally learned more of the language the following year after landing with the Boston Bruins, and my skills were honing well. Fear couldn't stop me and it shouldn't stop you. You may think that you can't relate to me, because I was a professional athlete. You may assume that you know what my life was like and possibly imagine it as being much more glamorous and easy than your own. I think you will be surprised at how similar we are and how many times I had to hit rock bottom or, simply face a daily fear, just like you do. My purpose helped me through that.

Really look at your life and outline when you were afraid but you kept plowing through. What was the result? Do you have any regrets where you let fear hold you back? What excuses have you given to others or yourself, when it was really just fear talking? Is fear in the way of your purpose? Let's look at how to get to that purpose next.

Bernie Parent with Michele Paiva & Dean Smith

Bernie Parent with Michele Paiva & Dean Smith

Chapter 3

Visions & Goals

When I discuss purpose, I explain that one cannot have purpose without a vision. More often than not, people get very confused by what a "vision" is. They ask me, "Bernie, is a vision something you see? Is it spiritual?" How did I get the success I have without knowing what a vision even is? Let me explain.

Purpose is not the vision. Your purpose is what you are meant to do, for that time in your life. Purpose can change as you evolve and grow. But each purpose seems to piggyback to help the next purpose. Do not think that if you have one purpose or many, that either is wrong. We are all different and our purposes are going to be as unique as each one of us. Goals are not vision. Goals are the stops you take to get to the vision.

Vision is the steps toward the purpose. Let me explain, as I know this may sound confusing. Let's say you are at the bottom of a mountain and you are looking up and see the cabin you want to stay at. You drove to the base of the mountain but now, the road has ended. You are faced with obstacles or opportunities, either way; it is not easy for you to just travel from point A to point B.

So, you look and have visions of how you will do this. You are in an almost dream state, envisioning what you will do. You are not envisioning just the purpose which is to get to the cabin but also the goals you need to get there. Goals may include taking a different route, moving boulders, flying by helicopter, taking the long way, charging through the brush, whatever. It doesn't matter because the goals are how you get the vision to become a reality, making the dream, which is the big picture of this; a goal and then, succeeding in purpose. Let me tell you a story that happened to me. It's not climactic but it was an "aha" moment for me after I realized what it was, and I hope it will be the same for you. One day I was out in the woods, hunting. It was cold, at least 30 degrees below freezing. I had been there a while and let me tell you, I thought my private parts were even frozen! I was not enjoying myself anymore, to say the least. I was distracted and was thinking, the heck with this, I'm going back to the warm cabin. Then all of a sudden, a buck was right in front of me! I forgot about being cold. My entire focus had changed. *Nothing* external changed at all. It was still cold, I was still cold, the cabin was still a hike away and yet, my focus was completely different. Because I changed my focus, I was able to almost ignore the fact that I was cold or, in other words, the negativity that held me back from my goal. This is how powerful the mind is; I was able to overcome the elements. Just think of what you can do if you just change your mindset. Here is what happened. I found my purpose again with a literal vision, the vision of the animal. However if you envision what you want, and keep that vision in you and alive, your purpose is easier to get to as the obstacles, such as for me in that moment, (i.e. the cold), become a background vision at best. The farther in the background the vision is, good or bad, the less power it has.

Bernie Parent with Michele Paiva & Dean Smith

If you are a negative thinker, the worst is always in front of you and is more your reality. If you are a positive and productive thinker, the positive is in your vision and is more your reality. When the buck walked in front of me; that was a physical vision that brought me back to my purpose, which was the hunt. The goals were to stay there and I did, but as I was cold and focusing on the vision of how cold I was, I was farther from my purpose and almost ready to turn around and forget the purpose or put it on a shelf.

Think about it. Really think about it.

How many times in your life have you lost vision, in your heart, and the goals seemed too hard or too menial, and you lost your purpose or put the purpose off. Think of the times you may have wanted to go to college or back to college to be "something else". Then you lost that vision and soon the small goals that needed to be met in order to reach that purpose seemed to be not worth it, just like sitting and being a little cold wasn't worth it to me. But if you suddenly had the opportunity to "be" that something, I bet you would if it wasn't too hard. You can't let obstacles or turmoil stop you from that vision. See your self, as you want to be. Gandhi stated, *"Be the change"* and that is very true. Be the change, but also be what you wish. In what ways have you lost vision of your purpose?

What can you do to reclaim your vision? Have you let an obstacle cloud your vision? If so, what is or was that obstacle and have you allowed it to remain, clouding your vision?

Bernie Parent with Michele Paiva & Dean Smith

If yes, why? If no, what did you do to remove it?

What steps could you take to remove that obstacle?
WOW

Chapter Four

Your Vision is Safe

Sometimes we confuse having visions with unsafe
territory. We are taught not to be dreamers. We are
taught to take the "safe" route, which is the "easy" route
actually. So, when you have vision and share it, people
may mock you or degrade your vision; and that
rejection is scary. Or, you may simply have been taught
that vision is not for you but for scientists and
innovators only, thus you stop your own vision because
you feel it isn't safe. Bull! Vision is safe! It is not only
safe; it is needed for your purpose. You need to
reincarnate yourself to a person who embraces vision, if
you don't already, because you need vision for purpose.
When you have a vision or a purpose it isn't always
immediate and it doesn't always come as simple as a
buck walking right in front like I had. Sometimes that
vision and purpose take years to reach, and sometimes it
is reached in a few moments. You can't be focused on
"if" it is working as then you change your focus. Losing
focus takes you farther from the purpose. If the purpose
is worth it, and you don't lose sight of the vision, you
will get there. Some people ask about my vision that
day, just days after Valentines Day when I lost my
eyesight on the ice. I tell them this. *Yes, I lost my career
but what I gained was overcoming an addiction through
a self-help program, and ultimately, being able to find
my more powerful inner wolf.* My life purpose was not
only to play hockey but also to be happy, and so, in
order for me to find that, I had to have the dark
moments to reach that purpose. It was a vision of mine

Bernie Parent with Michele Paiva & Dean Smith

to be happy and very fulfilled, and in losing a career, even one that was very good, I was able to get that purpose. My vision was clear in my heart, and so, it became real in my life. Vision sometimes shows you that you have to risk something to get to your purpose. Your dreams sometimes show you, by vision, that you have to sacrifice something good to get something even better. With our lives unfolding, some of this happens to us on the surface, where we do not realize that we are bringing it on, and in some ways it is intentional and we make those changes deliberately. A lot of us walk around and are not happy or even as happy as we could be. Some of us walk around years like this, even decades. It's really simple. If you are not happy, change the thing that is making you unhappy or the thing that is giving you results that are not bringing you happiness. When you take out the things in your life that are not working for you, your purpose becomes more clear as your vision of who you want to be or what you want to do, is that much more clear. Then, you bring your vision and dreams together to help you get the goals to make that purpose a reality. We all know people who did not have to lose eyesight to walk away from a career. This was their vision with intent. Sometimes that purpose comes from a deeper place that seems surface, similar to what happened to me. Realize that playing for the Flyers was amazing. I would do it again, and I loved it. However, my purpose is utilizing that time of my life and bringing a new purpose to the table for fans and others. This is my vision, to help others find purpose and be the best that they can be: to find their inner free wolf. You need vision for this.

Bernie Parent with Michele Paiva & Dean Smith

Chapter Five

The Unknown: Overcome Fear

We talk a lot about fear for a book meant to help you live without fear, don't we? Well, it's not empowering fear; it's taking the mask off of it so you understand it better. Once you understand it, you can use it to your advantage.

One of the things, one of the only things, that can put a stop to vision, the very roadblock to purpose and the obstacle of our goals, is the fear of the unknown. When I was in the woods and was cold, it was the discomfort and the unknown of what to do next that stopped my focus. If you filter all your excuses down which keep you from your goals, you will find that it is often the unknown, in some way, that is the true roadblock. When I was a kid, I was small, and probably over 200 people told me I wouldn't make it as a hockey player. I didn't care. I just focused on my dream, as at the time I did not understand the metaphysical behind it, but just focused on the dream and focused on getting to my dream. Now, in looking back, I see that I did not allow the negativity or the unknown, to stop me. Your mind is like the weather. The weather as a whole is flexible. Sure, in some areas it is always cold or always sunny; but as a bigger picture that weather changes constantly. Depending on where you are is how stable and how comfortable the weather is.

Now, think about this.

Bernie Parent with Michele Paiva & Dean Smith

The weather changes; the weather has seasons. We
expect it and for the most part we deal with the
unknown of a passing storm or a cloudy day, and enjoy
and appreciate the sunny, warm days. Our mind is the
same, like I said. Not all days are going to feel good or
be as productive. Sometimes you may be in a less than
great mood and that is OK. We have to accept nothing
but change. If you accept badness or negativity, you fail
to grow and see the better days, and the silver linings
behind the clouds.   Don't accept to the point of settling.
If you accept where you are, then you stop growing. A
lot of people seem to move a lot and are busy but are
stagnant in their thoughts. The "weather" in their mind
is like Siberia where nothing much changes and nothing
much grows. Why?

It whittles down to the unknown. They have, on some
level, a fear of the unknown. You can look at the
unknown and find it exciting or fear it. When you look
outside at snow falling, you can find it beautiful and
enjoy the change or complain. The minute you see it as
a negative everything in your day then is hampered as
you are letting something very external change your
mind and mood. If you accept change but flow with
change and the unknown then you have better things
coming to you.

I'll get back to the unknown, but first let's touch on
acceptance a bit more. If you just accept, you stop
growing, as I said, but the only thing you should accept
is change. If you can't accept change, then you will
resist change.

Change brings the unknown.

Bernie Parent with Michele Paiva & Dean Smith

Back to purpose… If you have no purpose you are active perhaps but you go in circles, because you have no vision or direction, and goals are not really goals but just randomness that you accomplish. Change becomes scary or fearful and at best, highly unwanted. When you have no purpose you want things to stay the same. You resist because deep down, not only do you fear but you have no ideas about what you want for yourself.

When you have vision, and you have direction, you embrace change. Change means exciting things will happen. People fear the unknown but so often it happens without them knowing it. As long as they are unaware, they are not afraid. But the problem with that is that they can't help direct it toward their needs. For instance, when you take a flight from Philadelphia to San Francisco, it is not a straight line. The airplane has to adjust constantly. On the airplane most people just think it is a straight line. Not so. Life is just like that. There are constant adjustments. When people don't like change or the unknown, they freak out over little hiccups in the mundane.

Yet people who embrace change see the little hiccups as typical things that happen to get from A to B.

Don't sweat the unknown but embrace it. Easier said than done, correct? Embracing a struggle, fear or an obstacle is not easy.

The trick to embracing this is to simply accept that each and every struggle is a process. If you don't like something, change it. Not everyone is going to be ready to make changes though; it's human nature to want to keep things safe and steady. Even psychologists will tell you that an abused person tends to stay with an abuser because there is a comfort level in being acclimated with the mundane, even if the mundane is negative, because the fear of the unknown is sometimes more fearful for them.

However, for each and every one of us, if we try to keep an open mind, we can take every struggle and decide when it's the right time to tackle that struggle. Be mindful of the struggles, and don't allow them to take a back seat in your life, because they will hold you back regardless of where you compartmentalize them. So, you have to be aware of struggles, and know that they are just a part of your process for growth and productivity. If you look back when you had to learn to tie your shoes or ride a bicycle, it was a small struggle, but as a child, you probably embraced it, saw it as a freeing experience and enjoyed the process. Well, do that with every struggle; it's all in your mindset. Embrace it.

When you know your purpose nothing is as scary. For instance if you suddenly wake up and are on an airplane, and you don't know where you are or where you are going, the unknown seems to be scary to you. You could have someone else on that plane and they know that the destination is an island or Disney World. They are not afraid even if the plane has to take a few other curves in the journey, because the small hiccups of unknown are exciting, not scary. This is life for the person with purpose. You can't focus on where you are but where you are going. Be happy where you are but don't accept it as "status quo".

Bernie Parent with Michele Paiva & Dean Smith

If I asked you right now, how would you feel if you died tonight, if you would look back and consider your life to be a success, what would you say? I'm not telling you what I feel about that just yet. But, think about it. There is an important lesson there.

First, let's look at how to embrace the unknown. Envision what you want with your purpose as the "carrot" to achieve, and the vision so how to get there, which may change off and on. Tackle the goals both small and large in your mind. Now realize that you are going to be like an actor in your mind. You are going to have the vision of "you" at your purpose. Play the part over and over. Allow change though, because you never know what may happen along the way.

Turn your back on safety and security. If fear knocks on the door, don't hide or pretend you are not home; which by the way is what you are doing when you run from fear. You literally are emotionally and mentally not "home" and you retreat into a very dark place where you are controlled like a dog.

Let the wolf open the door, and stare fear in the face. When you take risks, you don't always win. But you have to play to win, as they say in the lottery. You have to take risks and you may not win all the time or sometimes hardly ever, but you always learn from that and even in failure that is a win. Even in failing you shape experiences and your character and your ability to handle yourself. The more risks you take, the more chance of a win you have, and that win is beautiful. Each win is a beautiful thing.

Speaking of the lottery, I see people going into stores and buying lottery tickets and you know what? They are hoping someone creates change FOR them. Buying a lottery ticket is a very passive way to create change and it is not *you* creating change that much. The change you want to create should not be a gambling risk but a determined, well thought out risk. Risking is not the same as gambling.

People often shy from risk because they fear the unknown, and they fear what people will think if they fail. You can't do that. I took the risk as a skinny, small child and didn't care when people said I would never make it in hockey, and if I didn't make it in hockey I still wouldn't have cared, as at least I tried and enjoyed myself. We all have different levels of risk and sacrifices we can take every day. If risk is hard for you, start small. How you feel about yourself is going to be how you are seen; and if you love what you do, and risk comes along and you play it safe because fear is knocking, you lose out. Now back to my question. If you were to die, would you feel your life was successful?

Most people say, *"Yes"* and have a variety of assets they name to showcase why they were successful from materialism, to their families, to the legacy they feel they have left behind. Some people say *"No"* because they feel they haven't achieved enough yet on one or more levels.

However, the true answer is, you really don't know. You __can't__ measure your life. If you say yes or no, you are essentially accepting either you've done enough or you haven't done enough, and the reality is, you should be happy in the now, and should be focused on growth.

Your success is your reflection; nothing material, just how happy you are. Every successful person takes risks. There are a lot of things we tell ourselves, mostly through the nature of how we are taught through life to play by the rules, to stay in the box, to not rock the boat; that we are actually stopping ourselves from living well. We need to be happy in the now, but to be happy in the now; we have to be OK with having an ego.

An ego is a great tool and it depends upon how you use it. If you think of an actual tool, like a hammer, you would be abusing the tool by slamming it into a window and breaking the glass. You'd have a dangerous mess of glass shards. However, take that hammer and with control, and by using it properly, it can build a home. A home is not built when other homes crumble, but only when the proper items come together, properly meshed, to build a structure.

Your ego is the same; don't abuse your ego and end up with a dangerous mess, but use restraint and understand your ego is there to help build you up not shatter you or others. When you use your ego to break others down, you are not gaining anything, but instead, just becoming less of a pack member, and then, less empowering to your own life.

Bernie Parent with Michele Paiva & Dean Smith

I had a hard time with the Bruins and they had a tough year also. They were not doing well, and it was not unusual for bottles to be thrown at me during the game. It was common for "fans" to boo me, yelled awful things *to* me and *about* me, and I mean they did this if I was in the net or on the bench. In Boston Garden, it was easy for them to be passionate and emotional directly to us as they sat so close to us. It was an unknown, and it was something I had to deal with. Did I ever want to turn my back on hockey though? No. I took risks and don't regret it. I just kept being positive and that was my happiness.

Being successful is not even an issue and should not be your issue. Your answer should be that your happiness is the only consideration in your life; everything else revolves around that.

The wolf has a lot more of the unknown in the wild than the dog has in a locked up home, and the wolf is free.

In what way have you considered change?

In which ways do you embrace change?

In being very honest with yourself, how do you resist change in your life? Are there things you do that keep you from change and keep order in your life?

Is the order helping you grow or keeping you stagnant?

Bernie Parent with Michele Paiva & Dean Smith

Notes on your own fear:

Bernie Parent with Michele Paiva & Dean Smith

Chapter Six

Attraction

Loosely defined, "attraction" is the force by which one object attracts another. In quantum physics, it is essentially how we control energy. When people discuss attraction between each other, they often are really speaking of charisma and personality. By my definition, it is all of these things plus the ability to accept and go forward.

For me, when I think of attraction, it is the vibration of my mind. It isn't just how you act or your charisma, it is also how you control your energy, and what you anticipate and by force, the amount of energy you put toward that anticipation.

Think about it.

You can wake up and say it is a bad day. But is it a bad day? Millions of people are waking up and it is your choice to make it a bad day or not. So, if you think of it, how you live every moment is part of your attraction. If you go to sleep in a bad mood, thinking bad or negative thoughts, you won't have as peaceful of a sleep and on the chemical front; you are not doing your body any favors because bad thoughts and stress raise your stress hormones. But if you go to bed and think peaceful or happy thoughts, you are helping to calm your stress and ease the stress from your day; it melts away.

When you wake up, your outlook, like I said, is a choice. Let's say you wake up and decide it is a bad day and someone pulls out in front of you and then goes slow. You can curse the person and be miserable, or, you can realize we are all a part of this universe and take a different approach by saying, "Hey buddy, take your time, enjoy the morning."

You can take it even further and think, "Wow, he helped slow me down. He helped me maybe to avoid an accident."

A lot of people get mad at the person in front of them going a little slow but it is really themselves that they may be mad at. Maybe they should have gotten up earlier. Maybe they are just frustrated in life. Many people get mad at small things like a slow driver when, in truth, it is a big clue as to where they are in life.

Think of it this way; how you live your life and how you think is the roadmap to your life also.

If you wake up and have a poor attitude, *that* will be the roadmap of your day. Your day will follow how your mind works. It is not that hard to learn, but it is not learned overnight. It does take practice. Some people do it naturally, while some do not. How you were raised does factor into this as well.

We have the same habits from almost 200 years ago. I bet what you eat for dinner is really a potpourri of habits from your parents and grandparents, or whoever raised you, with very little variation. Well, mindset is the same way. Not everyone had "good habits" to learn in order to be positive and productive. Not everyone developed habits to find purpose or have vision. In fact, since I feel that most people are stuck and don't use attraction, it is my guess that our generations before us were as stuck as our own society.

Here is an example to put it into perspective for you. On January first, a lot of people start dieting or working out; getting ready for June, six months later, so that they can look good in their summer clothes. They know it will take about six months to get there. They learned from earlier generations how to cut back on overeating and how to increase exercise and activity. But for some reason, these same people want their mind and thought process to change overnight, even when they realize it should, or must, be done.

Restructuring the mind takes time.

When you restructure the mind, your ability to attract the energy that you anticipate and will help you achieve great things will begin to evolve.

One way to do this is actually both simple and difficult at the same time. Surround yourself with good people, and good places and good things will happen to you. Good people means people who are authentic, places as in spiritual or physical, and things, well that is any result.

At the same time, until you stop enabling the not-so-great people, you will find yourself surrounded with some bad people, and bad places and bad things will happen.

Bernie Parent with Michele Paiva & Dean Smith

It takes a lot to make your own changes. I used to hunt and fish with my buddies in Canada often, but their lives were surrounded by drinking alcohol. Being sober now for a few decades, I had to realize I had to walk away from that lifestyle. It wasn't a rejection of them; it was a rejection of that place for me. So, when I rejected that for me, I had to make changes and other people entered my life, and my place and, as a result, good things happened.

Like I referenced earlier, life is like an airplane, not really going in a straight line, and adjusting constantly to keep you on the journey.

Allowing attraction in a positive way is you being the pilot of your own journey.

The dog sits and doesn't have to adjust much, and has to deal with the people and place he is experiencing, as well as the result. The wolf constantly adjusts to the surroundings and is able to freely make choices to control his journey. He isn't making huge changes when he wakes. He anticipates and accepts the day, and what the universe brings him.

Chapter Seven

Acceptance

One can't actually have a true understanding and awareness of attraction without a level of acceptance.

If we refuse to accept, we will never anticipate all the good that the universe can bring us. For instance, if you get fired from a job or laid off, it is easy to feel rejected or fearful. You may have a jolt of pain in realizing you need to brush up on skills. However, this is an opportunity. Because now you are essentially free; free from constraints of a schedule and you can take at minimum your own time to create a destiny. It isn't going to be easy but you can acquire skills, or better yet, if you can, just take time to really think about what you want out of your life and now, with all of your time to focus on yourself, plan it and map it out to follow it.

I know what you are thinking. How can I speak about this so easily? I bet you think that I had it pretty easy barring that time in the hospital bed in darkness and at worst, losing my career.

Well, at one point in my life, I had nothing. I know some people knew about it, I mean, how could they not? But I didn't talk about it to anyone; it wasn't their business or their problem. I had to make a very hard choice and find myself, but I was in recovery and still healing, and for everyone's best interest, I moved to my boat. I made sure that my wife and kids still maintained their lifestyle. However, in order for me to maintain their life and heal, while figuring out my life, I was financially strapped. Suddenly, I was late on payments with the boat, and then, it was repossessed. I rented a room in someone's home, and lived on a jar of peanut butter and jelly and bread for the week as a norm of life. I stayed in my room for the most part and tried to evaluate my life. A lot was going on; I was trying to figure out my role in life, trying to figure out who I was without hockey being my self-image and the root of my sense of self.

It was all I knew of myself really from my early years and I didn't walk away from my responsibilities but I did have to take time and fit into my own role. Realize that in my life, even while married, I traveled most of the time. I was suddenly in a role without my career; that was new to me and not comfortable. Taking time for myself was incredibly important for my wellness, and for my personal growth as a human; to help me to be more productive. Yet, at the same time, I was in angst. I was living, in a way, without true purpose and just exploration that was tearing me apart. That changed though.

Something happened. One particular day, I got up and went downstairs. There had been a party and people were sleeping on the floor. It was at that moment that I said to myself, out loud I may add, "I'll never be in this situation again!" That was almost two decades ago, and I haven't been in that position since.

Bernie Parent with Michele Paiva & Dean Smith

I decided to look at the skills I had. I had none. Most people who are in bad situations actually have more skills than I do and certainly more skills than I had at that time.

If you are struggling right now, know this. You probably have more resources and skills than I did after winning the Stanley Cup. I had hockey but that was behind me now. I didn't have a college degree nor did I have skills or experience in anything. But the one thing I did have was contacts and relationships with people. I realized if I started introducing them, I would start to be able to make things work for them, thus make things work for me. I was able to get business coaching, learn from mentors and friends, take courses, was guided by others, and to become a businessman who was able to then help others.

If you feel you are at the end of your rope, in darkness and in a very bad place in life, all you need is to accept. Accept where you are but anticipate getting out of it. I do not care if you have no money, lost your house, lost your job, you still have tomorrow. It's a set back, not the end of the world.

Bernie Parent with Michele Paiva & Dean Smith

Bernie Parent with Michele Paiva & Dean Smith

Chapter Eight

Turning your Back on Safety

The title of this chapter may be sound somewhat radical. It may feel like it is the end of the world but it is not. In fact, it is an opportunity.

Ask yourself, what do you love? What would you love to do?

Take some time and really think about it; a day, a week, whatever time you can invest to do that. People assume their dreams won't work out, but remember that is their attraction energy that they are sending out. If they feel their dreams won't work out and they don't give their dreams focus and vision, then they certainly won't work out.

However, if you at least try you can say you tried and learned something from the experience. The worst thing that can happen is it won't work out; and if you don't even try, then the worst-case scenario is the same as a scenario where you didn't try! So, go ahead and you may as well try it and get something out of it, even if it is the beauty of living that dream in your mind for a while.

Just having that and experiencing it will not be something you regret, and you'll learn a lot about yourself, and probably learn even more skills. It's really a win-win even if you fail on the surface. Just take small steps and see yourself in that dream. Take control.

One other reason people feel very much in darkness and lack acceptance is that they are really living for someone else. What I mean by that is that they are afraid of what others will say, and live in a way that is more molded to the people in their life, be it a spouse or a boss. They are not showing who they really are 100%. If you live life that way, you are not living with true understanding of yourself and probably not understanding others.

However, if you start living for yourself, and if you accept yourself for who you are, others will accept you for whom you are. If they do not; so what. You need to be authentic to yourself.

When I was a kid, I would not accept what others thought of me. They thought I'd never be a good hockey player. However, I had accepted who I was at a young age, and even though I didn't fully understand it at the time, I wasn't letting anyone else mold me into his or her ideal of who I was to be. I would play the moves in my head over and over and on the street, I'd play hockey and put those moves from my mind to my physical body. I accepted who I was and anticipated the next step of growth.

There is no reason why you can't do the same thing. I've been up on the mountain, I've been in the valley and I've been through swamps, and I accept it all, and anticipate great things for myself still.

Like you, I had and have, family demands, and, in the past, a mixture of demands from my career. I've also been destitute and rock bottom, though this is the first time I'm publicly coming forward with that. It is part of who I am, and knowing this can be helpful and inspiring perhaps to you, that you can also turn your life around like I did. We will always have responsibilities but those responsibilities do not mean you have to stop being who you are. Accept who you are because once you are comfortable with yourself, and once you can anticipate the next exciting thing the universe brings you, the more you will be open to a more positive attraction that makes you happy spiritually, and in every other way.

The wolf doesn't pretend he is a giraffe, he accepts he is a wolf. He isn't sending out a wrong message to the universe and he is receiving the correct message to make this life the best it can be. Take a lesson from the wolf.

Bernie Parent with Michele Paiva & Dean Smith

Bernie Parent with Michele Paiva & Dean Smith

Chapter Nine

A Tool for Success: Socializing

There are many tools for success, only you may not realize that you own all of them. Just the fact that you are willing to learn or change is the best mechanism you could possess.

Not many people, in fact, only a handful of people, know that I have always been a painfully shy person. People assume because you are a sports celebrity, that you are outgoing and comfortable in crowds just because a camera may be on you. However, the truth is, if I were that much a people person at the time, I probably would not have been attracted to a career or life in an ice rink, rather, a career like teaching or marketing.

However, here I am today, a very different person, all because, at the turning point in my life when I went to the Flyers and asked for guidance, and they helped and directed me to mentors and classes, they also directed me into the art of socializing.

My tools if you recall, my instruments to help me accept yet to change my direction, were my contacts and relationships. Well, without being social there wasn't much that was going to happen between them, so I had to learn to be more social. If there is one bit of wisdom that I can give to anyone who reads this book, it is to be more social, and learn the art of socializing. It changes lives.

To add to attraction and energy, let me tell you a story about socializing that is very typical of my day. I try to make at least one person smile a day because I think it has a domino effect. Now to do this, I need to socialize in a positive way. I'm always authentic, which is a rule for me to live by that I hope you do also; be authentic.

Well, one day I was at a diner and I told the somewhat cranky waitress who was waiting on me in the crowded, busy lunch hour, that she had very pretty eyes. I don't think she knew who I was and I made sure she knew I was being authentic, not flirty. She grinned from ear to ear. I noticed after that, her entire demeanor changed and she was nicer to the other patrons that she waited on, smiling at them and being more sociable. In return, they also were smiling back. It was a domino effect and it only takes one person to start it. It doesn't always happen like that but you never know what a friendly comment to someone can do for his or her spirit, and sometimes it isn't something that shows up right away, but they carry with them.

Just as a mean, nasty comment can wear on us for years, a nice, friendly comment can lift our spirits for our entire life when we think about it. How about that? So, just for the sake of being nice, being social is a very compelling argument and it would be hard for anyone to debate that being a positive social being in our society could be doing anything but attracting wonderful energy. For me, being social was a tool I needed to learn; an accessory to my very being. For you, it is the same. Chances are you are not as shy as I was, but the fact is, you may not understand how important implementing sociable behavior is.

If you are more social, you talk to more people, get to share more, have more opportunities, and attract a higher energy. When I say higher energy, I mean positive people and situations, thus results.

To be sociable and positive, you have to be happy. That is authentic. So, if you are not happy emotionally, then you need to physically move. The body and mind are connected, so if one part of your being is not working as it should then get the other part to take over a bit to nudge it where it needs to be.

Think about that. If your body and mind are connected, then just changing your scenery can be helpful.

Don't believe me? Think about if you had to spend every day in a dark, cold, messy basement. Every day. Never see light. You probably would have a hard time being happy after a while and not be as positive socially at all. If you work in a cubicle and are unhappy with your work environment you may build resentment for your manager or peers. You may start to connect where you work with your level of happiness. Just change where you are even if it means just committing to a walk.

When you commit to changing your environment, you are taking control of your destiny, even in small increments, which is certainly better than nothing. I mean, think about it, you have a choice, to be miserable and sit in darkness, (and I mean darkness that is literal or virtual), or make a change to be happier. I choose happier!

OK, so now you are happier and you can be more authentic to be sociable. If you are shy, start small. Say hello or make eye contact with someone and smile. Start with people in your circle and expand to their friends and then to strangers. It won't happen overnight, and remember that I told you it could take a while; nothing should be expected to happen overnight. If it does great, but don't count on change that quickly. Your brain needs to redesign itself.

When you accept who you are and can anticipate being social, then you start to learn a trade secret of success.

Although you are a lone wolf, you are in a pack. The pack is always a bit stronger as there is safety and success in numbers.

Realize you need to want it. You may feel you are social enough but if change isn't happening and you feel stagnant, then meet more people. The key is you want to meet people who are headed toward, or are already in the place you define as "successful".

So, if you are a mother and want to be a better mother, then you start finding groups that help mothers by bringing resources and discussions. If you are a manager you may need to join business chambers. You may just want to visit a coffee shop and get to know people there. It doesn't matter how or when you do this, just commit and do it.

Bernie Parent with Michele Paiva & Dean Smith

Regardless of where you are, find places to meet people you can anticipate will support and raise you, not be an energy drag on you.

Your goals are to be free, happy and very successful, not to be depressed and stagnant.

People become stagnant sometimes because they have vision but not a plan of action; you need action to make things happen.

Socializing is action oriented, so you need to reach down into your spirit and find those tools to socialize. Even if you are going to be a bystander, go to networking events and learn by observation. But sooner, rather than later, start implementing what you observe. Remember, implementation or action, is needed for socializing. Socializing is what helps you to attract the right people, because if you do nothing, you get nothing. Now you may have to sift through people, but you'll soon figure out who wants to raise you higher and whom you can raise higher; it feels very natural and not like a chore. You'll now when it happens! Maybe it already has happened; if so, keep it going. "Domino" your energy so it comes back to you.

Everyone talks about "networking" and that to me, is so goal oriented. People "network" to get something out of the interaction. However, socializing is going in with no expectations other than getting to know others and sharing.

I have found, long term, that I "get" more out of socializing than out of networking. Being social is

Bernie Parent with Michele Paiva & Dean Smith

building relationships; networking is building a sometimes-meaningless business card collection.

We all do not have skills right off the top, but we all have the ability to reach into our toolbox and hone skills. We all have the ability to acquire knowledge, and part of that toolbox and source of knowledge is other people. Wolves are free, but run in packs. Socialize! Be a part of the pack!

Chapter 10

The Art of People, Places and Things

Everything really deals with three concepts: people, places and things. Throughout your journey, throughout mine, we will touch upon many people, visit many places, both concrete and abstract, and interact with things, which can take the form of gadgets, concepts or information. Here are some snippets that may help you develop your people, places and things to an art form, to better find and reach your purpose, or purposes in your life.

Dealing with Shame

Everybody has shame; if they say they don't, they are lying. The trick is to deal with shame properly. You may not be proud of what happened in your past but you have to own the fact that it made you who you are today. We all have crazy stuff or things that have happened; we all have made some poor choices.

Those poor choices though, have helped us to make consequent choices that were not poor. We learned from mistakes.

Accept your shame, and though it did happen, it didn't make you a bad person, and in fact, the very fact that you feel shame outlines you are actually a very good person probably, and you learned from that mistake. Once you accept the shame, you can look back as a new, improved and different person. Looking back with torment does not do you any good, but looking back with learned eyes helps you to discern your past and separate the behavior from you, the person, and learn and grow from it. Everybody has something they are ashamed of, so realize you are hardly alone in feeling shame.

False Illusions

I've heard so much about false illusions from people and here is what I have to say to that. So what. False illusions are a lot like dreams; allow yourself, in a healthy way, to embrace illusion, and use that creative tool as a springboard to help something else develop. Your illusions are just a part of your imagination; as long as you keep a healthy balance and use the illusions to help your purpose then you can embrace the dreams.

Time

In one respect, I can go on and on about how time is just a figment of human condition and get philosophical about time within the presence of the universe. The reality is that time is a form of measurement in people's minds. There have been studies that prove that as people age, the concept of time seems to go faster, and when someone is younger, time seems to go slower. Time is a concept of our brain, but how much of it exists, we really do not know.

For our purposes, time doesn't matter. You should plan for the future, anticipate the next moment with a positive outlook and learn from the past but the only thing that really matters is right now. So focus on "right now". The rest falls into place. As you focus on the now, when you reflect on this moment, it will be with more verve, and when you plan for the future, you will have a slew of positive moments to draw upon, if you focus positively on the now.

Ambition

Sometimes people have a blind ambition and though I do focus on helping everyone empowering himself or herself and finding their purpose as well as living their purpose, I cannot, and will not, tell you to be ambitious to the point of blindness.

Have you ever seen someone who pushes and pushes in one direction, be it a relationship or a career, and it just isn't working out? They won't give up. They are stubborn and they are going nowhere but downward. This is not determination and perseverance; this is blindness.

If something isn't working, change what you are doing. Maybe you are not following the right ambition if you have to work that hard at it and get nowhere. Allow yourself to be open to change. Ambitious people don't always win; and winners are not always ambitious.

Don't mistake ambition with serving your purpose and dreams.

Stress

We all have stress. We all have experienced it and
many of you experience it more often than you'd like.
Stress is your imagination playing tricks on you. It is
not always a bad thing; it often helps us to see what we
are doing isn't working. If we continue for instance, to
be blindly ambitious, we feel stress. Stress comes to a
head and we suddenly realize we are at rock bottom and
only then do we sometimes learn to create changes.
Change brings us to new directions and helps relieve the
stress. So, you see that stress can be a great learning
tool. A trick is to learn lessons from your stress and not
repeat behaviors.

If you give stress too much energy you are not giving
yourself empowerment but instead, being a victim to a
feeling. Take that energy and turn it into a tool to
empower yourself. You'll find that stress can change
things into positive, wonderful things!

Ego and the Pack

We talked about ego already; it is a tool that depends
upon how you use it; it can be dangerous or it can be a
positive mechanism that helps you to succeed and to
find inner peace and happiness. When you have ego, it
does not mean arrogance, and that is what people often
assume when we speak of ego. Arrogance is an over-
exaggerated sense of self-opinion, while ego is just your
personality or sense of self.

Bernie Parent with Michele Paiva & Dean Smith

When you surround yourself with other people who are part of a pack, that is, as we said, people who are helping you in your life or supporting your endeavors on many levels, as you do for them, then you have a healthy pack. You want to have a spiritual support system. Of course, your pack is large. It is everyone from the grocer to the person you may share your life with; however, the closer people are to you, the closer they are in the pack, the more their personality and your personality must mesh on more levels, including spiritually, socially, professionally and so on.

A great thing about the ego is that you can shape your psyche or your personality to be more external and not all about yourself. It is fine to be selfish but not overly selfish. One must care about oneself before one can care healthfully about others. It is a beautiful thing when you can get outside of yourself, and care about others and their egos, and to not only cultivate your pack, but cultivate their pack as well!

Life is not Fair

What do I mean by this? Well, it is as simple as it sounds. Life isn't fair. Some people will have more hardships and some people will have more opportunities handed to them. In either case, both people really do have a fair start. It's how you cope with, how you handle and what you do with what life deals you. So, is life fair? No, not always, but life isn't unfair either. It just is what it is; you make your path. No one really wants to hear that. People want to complain about life being unfair, but they only complain about that when they are not getting their way. You never hear someone win something big and then complain that life isn't fair.

"Fairness" is all about being unbiased. Well, in our world, we all have sets of rules, desires, what we, as a society, deem as important, and it continues from a large group of society to each individual. Fairness is very fickle in other words.

Life isn't really played by rules; we have a lot of political and ethical rules but in the whole, things are pretty wide open. Life isn't like a board game with the box top of directions and rules. Life is unfair, unreasonable and biased; and you are as unfair, unreasonable and biased as the next person. Just accept it and make sure that you live according to your own rules, without hurting yourself or anyone else. That's the best you can do. So next time you feel like life isn't fair, know that you are absolutely correct. How you handle the unfairness is far more important than if it is or is not.

Work

Life isn't about just being in the right place at the right time. You have to work at your goals, and you have to not be afraid to be a little vulnerable or take risks to get what you want, which hopefully is a part of the purpose of your life. It takes work, and sometimes it isn't

Bernie Parent with Michele Paiva & Dean Smith

enjoyable to get to your purpose. It's called "work" it is not called a "free ride". You may get a few free rides in life, sure. Great! However, there is going to be more work than free rides, so you better acknowledge that if you want to make changes as outlined, you are going to have to accept that work is called work for a reason; it is a lot of work! Work isn't bad. It is energy converted to action; and that often brings forth a result. So, if you spend your time procrastinating, you still get a result; the result is that nothing much is happening for you. If you spend your time eating too much, the result may be weight gain or health issues. If you spend your time working toward purpose, you will probably start to see results such as getting closer to your purpose. It's simple, but often avoided by those that don't like the word, "work".

Learn to like work, because life is often performance based!

Learn to Think More

Read, discuss thoughts with others, listen to talk radio, enjoy opera; do whatever it is you need to do, to learn to think more. Thinking is a skill and those that are not taught to think critically and positively are not going to be as versed at thinking, unless there is some natural talent hidden within them. It's just the way it is. So, my advice to you is that you should read and immerse yourself in a variety of outlets and hobbies, if for nothing else but to broaden your mind. I didn't say you had to enjoy all of them that much, just tap into different areas so that different areas of your brain are sparked, and create new paths of learning, thus, create more opportunities.

The great thing about our society now, as opposed to a hundred or five hundred years ago, is that we have the ability to share much more freely. We can hear an opera singer online, we can read great poets of yesterday and today at a library, we can have an online or telephone discussion with someone in a different part of the country or even in a different country altogether! We can travel easily, look at artwork from all over the world, and learn hobbies very easily. We don't have to be versed in any of this but we are most certainly stimulated when we partake.

Think about it.

We can, in one day, just using the Internet, view Paris, read poets, listen to the opera, check out sports in Brazil, call a friend in England and fix a meal using cacao beans from Mexico. We are in a place where we can learn something new every day, or several times a day. Embrace thinking, play games more, have lively discussions more, and learn to expand your world. When you expand your world, you expand your mind; when you expand your mind and hone your thinking skills, you are closer to your purposes. All of this is great, and I'm thrilled to share it, but I feel like I need to share a bit about myself so that you can get to know me more as your coach who will help you find your inner wolf.

Bernie Parent with Michele Paiva & Dean Smith

After this, we will bring this all together, and I will be a pack member for you so that you can go through your journey through risk and fear, find your inner wolf and create your purpose filled life. Here is a little more about me, a more personal story of where I've been and how I got to where I am.

Bernie Parent with Michele Paiva & Dean Smith

Part Two

Chapter One

Don't Fence Me In

This is going to be a little repeating of what I already discussed, but hear me out.

As you know, I was born in Montreal, Quebec, Canada. The youngest of seven children, I was born on April 3rd, 1945, the day before the Soviets liberated and drove out German forces during World War II. In the United States, songs that topped the charts were "Sentimental Journey" by Les Brown and Doris Day, and "Don't Fence Me In" by Bing Crosby and the Andrews Sisters. It was the same year that Canada became a founding member of the United Nations and in that year, Maurice Richard set a new record in hockey for the most goals in one season. My parents, Claude and Emilie Parent, gave us what they could; we didn't have a lot but we had each other and my parents were great providers always. We never felt poor though we were. I am not sure if it was just me naturally or those humble beginnings that prompted me to stare outside the window, dreaming, in my early days, of a different life. Dreaming was a habit for me; one that helped me to overlook the many people who told me I was too small to play hockey. I did not want to be fenced in by their

Bernie Parent with Michele Paiva & Dean Smith

words, and I refused to be; I refused to be locked up like a dog even in their mind.

As a preteen, I started playing hockey and enjoyed it and turned a deaf ear to negative comments. I kept my positive attitude going strong, and though I wasn't strong and lacked natural ability, I did have a willingness and determination to enjoy and excel at hockey. Early on, my parents were extremely supportive and helped me by believing in me and supporting my dreams; my father was a quiet man but had a work ethic that I respected.

 He worked for the Canada Cement Company and I paid attention to his quiet determination and strength. My mother was the nurturer and cheerleader. She was at all of my games.

I remember my early years when in Montreal, we had ice on the streets for months, and that is where we played. I didn't have skates so I had to be goalie with boots on; though even then, rich in imagination, I would imitate the moves of my idol, the great Jacques Plante, and how he played the game. It wasn't long before I was playing more organized hockey as a teenager. I did finally get a pair of skates but they were not goalie skates, because my family couldn't afford them. I did the best I could in them though, and truth be told, I didn't know the difference at the time and to me, hey, skates were skates! The first game I played was a nightmare. I knew it, the coach knew it and when I got home, my mother read my reaction to her inquiry about the game, and even she knew it. The coach told me he had to use someone else, and though I was saddened, it

Bernie Parent with Michele Paiva & Dean Smith

didn't stop me from skating and practicing; and my mother kept supporting me.

Oddly, a couple of weeks later the kid the coach used got hurt, and he called to use me as a replacement. I had practice a lot in those two weeks with the skates and this time, I had learned a valuable lesson already, even at that younger age. If opportunity knocks, go for it.

I did, and it worked out. I was a teen, enjoying being a goal tender, felt free on the ice, and that was my world.

Bernie Parent with Michele Paiva & Dean Smith

Bernie Parent *with Michele Paiva & Dean Smith*

Chapter Two

From Observer to Participant

In the 1960's, Hockey Night in Canada, one of the longest broadcasting programs that ever existed, lured over a million people weekly. It was broadcast on a Saturday night; also bath night. Realize, to save money, we had baths just once a week, which is why that memory sticks out to me so clearly. Anyway, millions of people tuned into to the program and I was one of them. I watched the program faithfully each weekend at eight o'clock in my parent's home, and watched my idol, Jacques Plante, play. I wanted to be just like him.

To add further to the dream, his sister lived next door to my parents, and he would visit her once a year; during this time I would hide in the bushes to catch a glimpse of him. I was incredibly shy, as a child and even into my adulthood, and I never said anything to him during those years, as I mentioned earlier in the book.

One thing I remember is that he smoked cigars; I'd see him with a cigar now and then. I smoke cigars now, and wonder if that wasn't something that I took up when younger because I aspired to be like him, again, as I already outlined. I don't want you to forget this, because it is important to realize how something seemingly small can be such a big deal to a kid, or to anyone with a dream.

Bernie Parent with Michele Paiva & Dean Smith

I remember that I really just looked up to him, in every way. Little did I know, as that gangly kid spying on him, that he'd end up to be a teammate of mine on the Toronto Maple Leafs in the future. You just never know what the future holds, and I firmly believe if you want something enough and work toward it, it does happen if it is what the universe has in its cards for you. But backtracking, there I was, just a kid. I remember one day sitting in a pew at church, and I felt a tap on my shoulder.

I remember immediately feeling concern that something happened to one of my parents or siblings. The man who tapped me asked me to step outside; and feeling apprehension, I did follow him. The man ended up being someone who worked with my father in the cement factory, and my father had talked to him about me. The man asked me to help out his Rosemont team, and I obliged. I was proud to be their goalie. We didn't win that first year but I vowed that we'd win the next year; and as I often do, I put my mind to it and plowed ahead. We did, in fact, win the following year. Still just a kid, I was making a name for myself as a goalie in the city. I had gone from mostly observing hockey and dreaming, to participating.

Bernie Parent with Michele Paiva & Dean Smith

Chapter Three

Transformation

Here I was, a 16-year old boy, still a child. I was drafted by the Boston Bruins; but it was right after I had a tryout with the Junior Canadians who told me after five grueling days of tryouts that I simply didn't have what it took. I remember walking in the door and my mother asking me how the tryouts went, and I remember telling her "not so good". I laughed and she was fairly silent, knowing what I meant. She knew I was rejected.

However, that was all right before the Bruins. Now realize, at the time the Boston Bruins were really not a great team in the early 1960's. I was drafted out of junior hockey that year, and it was that year that they finished last. I was out of Montreal but not owned by the Montreal Canadians, and I was one of their first picks.

Right after this time, I was assigned to the Niagara Falls Flyers; do you see a trend? The "Flyers" name would follow me for most of my career. This may seem exciting but realize for a kid of sixteen, it was scary. I was a child still. Think about it. I had to leave home and leave my French-speaking region to an English speaking region. I didn't even know the language, and I was a kid away from his family! I left my family behind, and off I went. It is still extremely hard to talk about, experiencing the fear I had as a kid, hopping on a train and heading to Niagara Falls.

Bernie Parent with Michele Paiva & Dean Smith

In keeping with all the fear and risk I talked about earlier; not many individuals have to deal with that much fear and risk in their lives, much less as a child. But I did because, at the time, more than anything, I wanted to play hockey. A big problem was that the team I had been drafted from was being quite hard to deal with. They wouldn't release my equipment so, I didn't have my goaltending equipment and wasn't able to play, needing to stay on the stands for about a month while I waited and waited for them to release and send it.

The frustration of waiting for the equipment was one thing; the frustration of not being able to communicate was quite another. I think the letters back and forth to my eldest brother, Jack, are what kept me going; and I get teary just thinking about that time frame in my life. He kept me grounded and feeling connected. Like I talked about before, one can be a lone wolf but you have to be a part of a pack. At that timeframe, the team was a pack for me but my family served as my steadfast pack: my safe den.

In that time frame, I had to learn a lot and learn it quickly; including the names of certain foods, how to communicate in English and so much more. Realize during all of this, I haven't much talked about lessons. I really had no formal education in playing hockey; however, that was about to change. While some people have a teacher or family friend to mentor them, I had a coach, Bill Long. As a late bloomer, he helped me to understand angles; there I was, a junior hockey player just learning about angles on the ice. Realize the next

step was becoming a professional; so you can see just
how much of a late bloomer I was.

Late or not, we ended up winning the Memorial Cup
Finals. That is the next best thing to the Stanley Cup.
Realize that though I was only in Niagara for two years,
we had a short period of time to perform to win it, and
we did it.

It was during this time, that I was expanding and
transforming and I didn't even realize it, even in spite of
injuries, including a broken thumb, where the bone
went right through the skin. It was a time where I was
so in the moment and focused on fulfilling my goals
and dreams that I didn't realize I was working toward
my purpose.

Bernie Parent with Michele Paiva & Dean Smith

Bernie Parent with Michele Paiva & Dean Smith

Chapter Four

Anticipation

As you read a little about my life, you'll start to see that
I was applying my philosophy long before I realized it
was even a philosophy at all, and I had no idea it was
something that I could explain and share. It was just
how I lived; and I realized much more than this many
years later. Everything was stacked against me at the
Boston Bruins' training camp as they already had two
goalies; Eddie Johnston and Gerry Cheevers, and they
were both great players. Oddly, just five weeks into the
season, when I was in the Minors, I got a call that both
Johnston and Cheevers had gotten hurt and I was flown
to Chicago where the Bruins were playing. I was in
shock; there I was in Chicago Stadium, further proving
the power of a dream. I had wanted out of the minors
and Oklahoma so badly, and wow, there I was in
Chicago, in my first game in the NHL.

I remember the crowds cheering and that famous organ,
which at first was great but after a while I could have
blown it away with a gun had I the chance because it
was so loud!

There were details about that game that escape me, and
some that stick out to me; but neither here nor there, the
point is, I was there. I did it and we tied. I remember it
was a hard game, harder than I had imagined it would
be. It was an honor, and when I look back, realizing that
there were only 120 players in the NHL at the time, and

I was one of them, it was not only an honor but it felt like my destiny. I was part of Boston; a great city with history and also a young atmosphere with the colleges and universities. It was a great place to be.

As great as it was, I had weaknesses and the fans knew it. The second year was tough; and the fans not only let me know it but they expressed it a little too well! They'd boo me, throw bottles at me even, both on the bench and while I was in the net. I tried to think positive and productively though; these were just passionate fans who wanted the best for their team, the Bruins.

I tried to understand them but part of me wanted to escape them; and I'd even fantasize about Oklahoma City and my minor days, as much as I loved the NHL and Boston. I didn't quit though, and I kept moving ahead steady and refused to let anything get me too far down; and just did the best I could.

I wasn't coping as well as I could have, and this is when my already-in-place drinking habit became a flourishing coping skill that was, in the end, as expected, unsuccessful.

I was escaping, not coping and at that point there was also talk about the NHL expansion, and I didn't know where I was going to end up. That open opportunity was a little fearful but I looked at it with anticipation, as thus far, every opportunity kept leading to better and better doors opening.

Bernie Parent with Michele Paiva & Dean Smith

Chapter Five

Freedom

Well, once in the original six (leagues) of the NHL, I was now chosen by the Flyers, one of the expansion teams. At the time, remember I was not from the country, and the expansion teams were going to be in Philadelphia, Minnesota, St. Louis, Pittsburgh, Oakland and Los Angeles. I didn't even know where some of these locations were, so I was wary. I remember when I found out about the Philadelphia Flyers; I had been playing golf, and my first reaction was disappointment. Then, I started to realize what Philadelphia was; it was the home of Freedom for the United States. It was all about the Liberty Bell, Ben Franklin and more. I was suddenly seeing that this could be a home for me.

Like I have said earlier, in some of the darkest moments come the best opportunities.

In hockey, sometimes in your greatest defeat comes your greatest victory and that is what happened when we got the crap kicked out of us during the playoffs one time. At that time, I remember that we were told we'd never get beat up like that again.

We didn't. Management was moved around, players were coming on board that worked well with us and complemented us, and we were being prepped to compete for the Stanley Cup. It wasn't easy that second

year; obstacles were plentiful and we had to overcome
them.

There were no goalie coaches in those days, and I was
still inexperienced comparatively speaking, so I didn't
have enough resources to help correct myself. There
were other people like Doug Favell, who I felt was
more physical and could make a save from his athletic
prowess. I didn't felt that I had that to fall back on.
Additionally, I had my own style; I never thought to
completely change my style, and I felt I had to take time
to turn my own style into something more concrete to
make my game turn around.

As time went by, I worked hard and our team was going
into other seasons with more trades. Then, there was
something huge; I was traded to the Toronto Maple
Leafs. In the hockey world, it was a blockbuster of a
trade, but to me it was like an atomic bomb went off. I
was leaving my team, my friends, and my life, all
behind. If a photo is worth a thousand words, then I
have a photo that speaks volumes. It's of me, standing,
saying goodbye to Philadelphia and heading to Toronto,
with tears in my eyes, and in my eyes, was fear. I faced
the fear though, and had to risk all that I loved and felt
comfortable with. It was not the first time, and I knew I
could do it again.

As I packed the car with my wife and our infant son,
Bernie, Jr., we ran into an awful snowstorm. We were
driving in the well-known Snow Belt area of New York
State, and found a hotel to stay at until the next day.
Carol, my wife, stayed upbeat throughout this and she
was the one who stayed upbeat about the move. We

Bernie Parent with Michele Paiva & Dean Smith

moved ahead and did so with determination, and it felt freeing to do that.

In those days, a lot of fights broke out on the ice. One particular game when one did, my mask was thrown from the ice to the crowd; it was the only mask I had at the time. I was saddened because I knew I couldn't go out and play until I had a mask. The next morning, at around 8 o'clock, there was a knock at my hotel door. When I opened it, I was shocked to find a man and his young son, probably about twelve years old, holding a mask. Not my mask but a mask all the same. The father and son stated that they knew I needed a mask, and were offering the son's goalie mask, to me. I was really moved by this. Though I didn't take the mask, I made sure to get them tickets for the next playoff game. They really understood the need for the goalie mask.

In all of this, please realize how many pack members there were in my life, be it my wife who helped me to be determined to plow ahead and or a stranger and his son offering a much needed piece of safety equipment. There is a freeing feeling when you realize that you are not alone but also not smothered.

There are other times you just feel free. I got to play against my childhood idol, Jacques Plante. I felt uneasy playing against him and yet it was like the master playing me, the pupil. He was a genius and he stood up for what he thought was right, without wavering; that is pretty powerful stuff.

Bernie Parent with Michele Paiva & Dean Smith

I got to know him as a player and as a person, and learned a lot from him by observing and talking to him. I actually asked him to teach me to perfect my game, not knowing what kind of response I'd get from him. Without hesitation, he said yes. He'd help me. The words he spoke to me that stayed with me was that he wanted to teach me but that he wanted me to keep my own style; that if you try to emulate someone else too much, it wouldn't do any good. He knew that the pack was important but that the power of the inner wolf was even more important, just as I learned.

There is something very freeing about your idol telling you to keep your style, confirming that who you are, is plenty good enough all along.

Bernie Parent with Michele Paiva & Dean Smith

Chapter Six

Risky Business

In that time period, the World Hockey Association, the WHA didn't seem as authority-worthy as the NHL. I didn't realize I'd be a part of history when they started talking and making noise about taking some NHL players and so on. Some of the NHL teams got hurt worse than others by the time the WHA was through; as they pummeled through grabbing their players with quickness and weight.

So, I flew to Miami, signed my contract for the Screaming Eagles and the next day, they folded and then became the Philadelphia Blazers. I was confident. I had honed my skills, and even had my childhood idol as someone who helped me tweak my skills. I was actually making history as the first NHL player to jump to the WHA, and though I was still the same shy Bernie Parent, as far as hockey was concerned, I was not the same shy, insecure kid who was playing junior hockey not that long before.

Well, to add to the twist, I broke my ankle that first week and was in a cast for six weeks. Things were different in the WHA. They didn't have as much money and though some of their contracts with players were high dollar, they skimped in other areas. For instance, the NHL flew us everywhere we went for the most part, and we stayed in great hotels. The WHA used buses and we stayed in hotels that were not nearly as nice. With the WHA, it seemed it was all about cutting corners at that time. However, there is always a silver lining; in the WHA they played offense first and defense took care of itself for the most part. That meant I was very active in the games and some games I had fifty shots at me. I was able to really hone my skills and apply what I learned from Plante, my genius idol. Ultimately, it was the bleak financial situation of the WHA that made me walk away, and I fully knew I'd get hit by the press and even some team-mates. I had to take that risk though and I had to focus on my journey. I was upfront with everyone and I was focused on my journey, without hurting anyone along the way. I had a family and responsibilities and nothing was going to stand in my way.

Bernie Parent with Michele Paiva & Dean Smith

Chapter Seven

Consequences

When I decided to return to the NHL, it was with careful planning and a lot of hope. I was worried not only about getting back to the league but also how I would be welcomed, or rather, *if* I would be welcomed, with open arms or shunned. My agent was already working on a deal with the Flyers and sure enough, that is where I landed, with the orange and black, in the City of Brotherly Love, where I wanted to be. I was thrilled when the new coach, Fred Shero said to me, "I don't know anything about goal tending, and you are on your own". That is just what I wanted to hear! "To be able to make it my own." Being a goalie is of course, part of a team but, you have to do a huge job as an individual as well. It's a unique place to be; I credit my time spent training with Jacques Plante as a turning point for me that helped me make myself both solitary with my own style and still a fraction of the big picture which was the team.

I was given the number "one" jersey and it meant a lot to me. It meant that the team thought I was their number one goalie. Talk about set back and fear; listen to this. During my first game back, I was being compared to Doug Favell, who was athletic and made everything look exciting when he saved. The papers tried to build me up, but there I was in front of 18,000 people, and I let in eight shots in the first ten minutes. Talk about fear.

Bernie Parent with Michele Paiva & Dean Smith

I was pulled out of the game; what a setback. I wasn't in shape, and I wasn't ready; but I kept working at it and the Flyers were a special team. They were a tough, but not a dirty team in any manner. It was a good team of guys who could skate and score, but we had some guys who could fight when needed. We were a little different in that we were a tougher team. Some teams just skated and played the game, while we could do it all if need be.

Fred, the coach was like a compass leading us through the woods. He helped give us direction and he made the Flyers special.

We went on to win the Stanley Cup not once, but twice. We had a lot of people around us, including our own selves, to put plans into action and to overcome obstacles. The first time we won the Cup there was an overwhelming feeling. There was even a parade for us!

During the second big win, I felt more focused than ever in my entire professional hockey-playing career. While we played Buffalo in the first game of the Cup finals at the spectrum, I stopped every shot. It wasn't just about the players or coaches; it was the crowd. The crowd is a part of the experience. When I would hear the crowd "oooh" or "ahhh" when I'd stop a shot, it was like it gave me energy and I knew we had it going on. I'd be in a zone, but I'd be connected to others and they were connected to me.

Bernie Parent with Michele Paiva & Dean Smith

There was no such thing as a key player in the games though; as often people asked me about this. The coach, Shero, would say the same thing. Everyone, regardless of how long they are in the game, is a key player. There is no hierarchy.

That is how it is in life. Someone can be around you your entire life and you can meet someone for ten minutes. Both people can change your life dramatically and both are equal in terms of how important they can be to your purpose. That is not the same as forging relationships but it is in terms of who is a key player. Everyone in your life is a key player.

Again, it's about the pack, and it is about being a wolf. It's about risk, fear, purpose, vision. It is all here. When you are looking at my life, the situations are different but the components are really the same as your own life. Apply them. Everything results in consequences; it is up to you to decide which consequences you desire.

Bernie Parent with Michele Paiva & Dean Smith

Bernie Parent *with Michele Paiva & Dean Smith*

Chapter Eight

Light and Dark

The next months were not as climactic; I had a severe neck injury. As expected, I had many hits and injuries in my career and I do believe it was an accumulation of those injuries where an underlying weakness crept up. I moved a certain way, and suddenly my right arm went numb and it felt like someone had stuck a crowbar into my neck. I was in the hospital almost two weeks before it was finally decided after much manipulation, stretching, discomfort and testing, that they needed to remove a disc from my neck; that rendered me out of service for most of the 1975-76 season. Things were not the same then as they are today; there wasn't technology or support for players and there was not anyone working on rehabilitation with me either. Because of this, when I felt pain when in rehabilitation, I didn't know if it was a pain I should be feeling and a natural healing process or something that was doing me more harm.

I also was aware while on the ice that the next hit could kill my career and give me years of pain. Regardless, I managed to get back to the season to play. To add to the frustrations, I wasn't in shape enough to help carry the team to playoffs, and I remember I did very little and spent a lot of time on the bench. Even though I was dressed and there, I did not feel connected to the team at the time because all I wanted was to be out there on that ice.

Bernie Parent with Michele Paiva & Dean Smith

The next season was a little better; I needed to connect with someone who could help me though. I needed to be more a part of a pack. We got in touch with Plante who had since retired from the game and he immediately was able to identify my obstacles, and he worked with me. He was like magic. He was the greatest goalie and I'll always be grateful to him.

I felt great and was thankful but Philadelphia didn't get the Cup that third year. It was just four years after our second Cup win that I suffered my eye injury.

The neck injury and the eye injury are what most people know of my plights. However, sugar and alcohol are obstacles that I had to overcome as well. One could have killed me, one I simply don't need anymore. I've been sober for thirty years.

Remember that I told you before that I had hockey as my self-image. It was how I communicated myself and how I communicated with others and often, how others communicated toward me: through hockey. When my self-image changed, when hockey was not my job or my life, I was at a loss. As I have said several times already, it was all I knew from a very young age, and even my idols and family life had rich hockey memories, from watching Plante visit his sister to broadcasts on Saturday nights with the family. It was in my blood.

A self-help program to deal with alcohol saved my life. It was only then that I stopped using alcohol to numb me and to hold me up, like a crutch.

Bernie Parent with Michele Paiva & Dean Smith

Even as early as my junior hockey days, I was using alcohol to deal with travel and transformations, obstacles, and fears; you name it. Even boredom. I was young, going out with the guys on the road, having some drinks with the guys just for something to do. Throw in that I am a naturally compulsive person. I didn't realize the habit was creating a problem in my life until it was a problem that I needed help to overcome.

Oddly, even with my wife and children trying to help me a few times, once I was sober I realized that the booze never solved a single problem.

Then one day, I left saying I had to go to the store. I came back three days later, couldn't find my car, and had to get a cab home. I remember walking in and sitting down; my wife and kids said nothing. It was very sad. I went upstairs and went to bed for a while. When I woke, I felt like angels had come down and helped me get the courage to call a self-help program. That was 1980 and I've been sober ever since.

It wasn't easy. I had to change my entire life; I had to immerse myself in the self-help program and the people. You get what you attract; remember that on the road with hockey I'd drink. In the summer, I'd meet up at home with friends and socializing with them also involved alcohol. So, I had to make changes and walk away from people who drank socially all the time, for my own health.

Remember that I am naturally shy, and, at the time, painfully shy. I had to force myself to make new friends and change my direction.

Bernie Parent with Michele Paiva & Dean Smith

One story has little to do with women and more to do with the alcohol. I was judging a contest of cheerleaders and the women were, yes, beautiful but I was invited to go to party after that would have "plenty of booze". I remember being frozen with fear, after only being sober for about two weeks at that time. That is when I went to my sponsor's home and there I sat on the steps for two hours, in fear, shaking and not sure I could hold out. I did, and I won my first battle with alcohol.

Sometimes you need that darkness to compare it to the light. Sometimes you can't understand how much light you have in your life until you experience the darkness as well.

I had to learn to drive myself to parties so I didn't have to be around someone who was drinking, and I did so to be responsible for myself. I remember people, even teammates saying "Oh you don't have a problem" and, at the time, I realized that they may have had a problem and just didn't realize it just like for years I didn't realize it. When I started taking inventory of how often I had alcohol in my life, even when home, it was painfully apparent to me that alcohol played a bigger part in my life that I had expected even when I was first sober. The more I learned, the more I was aware.

Sugar was a little different. I tried giving it up more than thirty years ago and didn't; but then I've been without sugar for almost a year now. One time, about twenty years ago, I had cut out sugar mostly from my life and one Easter I went out, bought a chocolate bunny

Bernie Parent with Michele Paiva & Dean Smith

and proceeded to eat the entire thing. That one actual day changed the last two decades for me.

What I thought was just a one-time thing, really became a pattern that I had a hard time controlling until recently.

When I look back at my hockey career, it is like a series of mountaintops, with peaks and valleys. You look at the landscape and you see a landscape, but it is made up of highs and lows; without the highs and lows, the contrasts, it isn't as beautiful. Life is like that, highs and lows, darkness and light.

Everything I base my life on revolves around people, places and things, as I said earlier in the book. If you are hanging around a bar at two in the morning, look around. Is this what you want from your life? Take a quick inventory of your job, your relationships, or what things you have in your life; is this what you want for yourself? It not, change it. You can't have only darkness in your "people, places or things" if you want to experience light.

Bernie Parent with Michele Paiva & Dean Smith

Bernie Parent with Michele Paiva & Dean Smith

Chapter Nine

The Wolf

I consider myself a wolf, and you should consider
yourself the same. The "wolf" is known as the father
and brother to the dog. It is the quintessential wild and
brave animal, and is often the model of efficiency and
loyalty. If misunderstood, the wolf is feared, but only
for a short time, until those around the wolf see him for
who he is. Wolves are authentic, and run in what is
known as family packs as well as unrelated packs
numbering in the dozens. Unlike a dog, a wolf is
sustainable to live in rough environments, and
independently along with the pack; being both protected
by and protector of their pack. It's a balance to survive
and thrive. Unlike a wild animal that knows their place
in nature, as people we often have to filter the
distractions and ask ourselves "who are we?"

I had to do this myself after my career, and during
recovery. I would look in the mirror and didn't know
the guy looking back. Bernie, the player, was done; but
what else was there? I didn't know. I knew I was an idol
to some; one person in particular was Pelle Lindbergh. I
worked with him a bit when I was a goaltender coach
for the Flyers. He was a great kid and I had the honor of
awarding him at the NHL awards. There is a photo of us
at the Wachovia center in Philadelphia holding the
award.

Bernie Parent with Michele Paiva & Dean Smith

I remember he stated something to the effect of having fifty years in front of him that night. Well, at two in the morning I got a call. He had been in a car accident and by the time I arrived at the hospital, he was on life support. He died shortly after that. I have never forgotten him.

You never know the difference you can make in someone's life, and it is incredibly important to me to know I make positive changes in people's lives, be it whether I coach them on or off the ice. I am lucky to be coached as well; the Flyers have been a huge part of my life on and off the ice also. It was the Flyers who introduced me to the world of business.

It wasn't easy because I had no background and at 35, I was starting all over again. Perhaps I was ahead of my time, because people today are often changing their careers at ages 35 or 40, from desire or need. For me it was both need and desire.

I lost everything when I lost hockey, or so I thought. I had to rebuild and through books, observation, mentors, studying and trial and error, rebuild I did. I had to slowly develop a new pack, and slowly transform into a wolf.

I had to learn that unlike in hockey, when I did a job well done, there would be no cheers from the crowd, and summers were for work, not time off. My entire life was unique and I embraced these changes. What I found was that business was a lot like hockey. You observe the masters, you keep your style, you make tweaks and changes and you play by the rules but do

Bernie Parent with Michele Paiva & Dean Smith

your best. I had to overcome a fear of public speaking;
and I did it with the help of a psychologist, Dr. Bob
Hackinson. Playing in front of 18,000 people was easy,
but speaking to a small crowd even, was frightful.

But I looked past fear, took the risk and had the vision;
and I did it. What got me through hockey was
discipline. That is what you need to get through your
goals to your purpose as well. Just commit and have
that discipline.

With that comes changes though; I remember when I
was trying to find myself, and really get in touch with
who I was to find my purpose. I had a 41-foot Viking
boat; and I remember saying to my wife and kids that I
wanted to go spend time on the boat to find myself,
alone. I said I'd be there for them but I needed some
time alone. Carol said it wouldn't last and I'd be back. I
asked if they wanted to go with me, and they all said no;
even the dog walked away from me. So, I left, and I
never did return. Who I was, was not someone happy
with the life I had set up. Carol and I ended our
marriage amicably and have remained very close as I
am also with my children and grandchildren. I treasure
all of them. We are all very close and, in what seems
like the biggest defeat, you can have your biggest
victories. The darkness moves and suddenly there is
light.

Not everything you do is going to be the best decision,
but you can't regret it. Sometimes playing it safe feels
right or feels good but, if you miss opportunities to be

the best you can be, you are holding yourself back.
You've got to take risks. In my hockey career and even
in my earlier business days, I felt like a dog learning
how to jump a fence; just going through a move. It
wasn't until, if you think back to my experiences, that I
had more freedom, that I was able to be the best I could
be.

Sometimes you have to take risks. Maybe you will lose
it all. Many times risk takers lose things once, twice, or
three times over even. But each time there is a reason it
happens. You keep moving and going on and you
realize that with risk is loss but there are also wins that
you simply can't obtain by playing it safe. You won't
feel the win of stopping a shot in the net until you are
on the ice blocking the shot. I talked about how I lived
in a room and ate peanut butter and jelly out of
necessity. It was the school of hard knocks, or a
learning curve as they may say today. I've seen the view
from the mountaintop and I've tasted swamp water. I've
been in light, and I've been in literally and figuratively
darkness as well.

Regardless of where I was, I had dreams. When you
dream, you make better decisions. There is a
peacefulness that comes over you. It's even a common
phrase from a parent to a child, "Sweet Dreams" before
bed. It's because dreams are a pleasure, and you should
embrace them. Act upon them. Dream of the wolf
within you and where that wolf wants to roam.

Bernie Parent with Michele Paiva & Dean Smith

Chapter Ten

Exist or Thrive

To exist is to settle. To thrive is to live. In a hospital when a baby is not doing well or a child is not growing according to medical needs, they call it "failure to thrive". We are meant to thrive, to live.

Life is about living; not every moment is going to be beautiful. Sometimes people live someone else's dreams. They work for a company that they do not respect, in a job that doesn't challenge them or bring them joy. They are told how long they can vacation and their income based on a standard, not on their ability, which dictates their home and "things". They call it security. But that same company can lay them off and they live in fear of being laid off or let go. They don't want to rock the boat or bite the hand that feeds them so they take the disrespect and lack of fairness, and curl up like a good dog and not bark.

If that is your dream fine, but you should be living so that you love your job and career; that you have purpose and enjoy the life carved by *your* decisions, regardless of what that life is. What works for you may not work for your neighbor; be happy with what you have and who you are and don't compare yourself. There is something I call the Universe. Others call it God. The Universe is constantly in motion. The earth is in constant motion every year, every month, every day, every hour, every minute and every second. The Universe is huge and we create it with our mind;

without our mind it wouldn't exist. After something happens, people look up in the sky and say "thank you, God." It is within us, though.

I think most, if not all, people today feel that they have had some kind of spiritual happening in their body, or observed in some way something spiritual, at one time or another. An example of this is a story I've heard where a woman, who may not have been more than 100 pounds, picks up a full-size car under which her son was trapped. Where did she find that inner strength? Where did that power come from? Ask the woman and she will not know.

It was the power of the Universe that she had within her all along, without realizing it. The power to be happy is also within us. Smiling and being happy does not mean we don't have problems, it means that we have the ability to create our own happiness despite our problems.

Happiness comes from within; it isn't as external as you may think. I can remember being on an expensive boat, with a lot of money and technically, fewer problems. I was not always so happy in that position. However, I remember many times where I was in a small, used canoe, and had a lot of problems in my life, and I could be very at peace and happy. "Happy" is from within and once you figure that out, you can change a lot of your life just from that powerful tool. Places are important but they are often a state of mind, rather than a geographic location. Luckily, I thank God that I never had a job in my entire life, or at least felt like I had a job. A job is like a chore, but what I have done, including any businesses I am involved with, are enjoyable to me and a part of my life on a personal level. To call them jobs would demean them.

I didn't write this book to just talk about myself; there is a goal here. I want each reader to not ever have to say "what if". I want each reader; you, to dream and reach for those dreams. Sometimes getting the dream isn't as important as the process of achieving. It's getting there and experiencing it as a reality, even in part, that creates the most growth. It's where you learn skills, cope, enjoy and where you lose track of time and space. I wanted to take this book though and be able to outline some of my life, so you can better understand me, to learn from my mistakes and to also see how I coped in positive, productive ways.

Find out what you love to do and then dedicate your life to that love. Maybe you have a few loves; whatever it is, be it one thing that seems silly or a million outlandish dreams to others, just go for it. Never let a dream die. Never let darkness win.

How do you find what you love?

When you find what you love, and experience it, there will be no darkness. It's all about light in love.

It's not just about you; it's about people. I'm honored that I had the people in my life, especially the Philadelphia Flyers that I was able to work with, work for and align myself with. Be it from the Bruins, the Flyers, the man who tapped my shoulder while I was in church so long ago, or the letters from my brother Jack; I have memories that I really feel were beautiful.

I am mentioning these experiences so you can fully understand that through the darkness there was so, so much light. You have it in you also, and my hope is that as you reflect on yesterday or on fifty years ago, you can have the same warmth and fondness that I do right now. I'm focused on tomorrow being a memory for the next day after; my life is a never-ending quilt of lightness now.

I've come a long way from the scared boy traveling miles from his family yet, as a fearful man in darkness in that hospital bed, I felt like that same scared, young boy.

I felt fear traveling in the snow in upstate New York with my wife and baby by my side.

In my life, I've been dropped into an area not being able to speak a language, almost frozen with fear of freezing to death, and literally blind to life. I've used alcohol to escape and woke up from depending upon sugar. I've been humbled by wearing a "thirty" and I've been honored to wear a "one".

I've written letters to my brother that still make my eyes well with tears. I wouldn't change a thing. The road wasn't easy but it has been my road, and in the end, it's been filled with mostly light. My ultimate hope is that long after I'm gone from this world, my ideas will carry on for several generations to come. And that people all over the world will carry on those ideas. That is a dream that I can see now.

We all have darkness around us, but finding the light within illuminates our dreams and realities. I am not ready to dim this light anytime soon. I just want to share it now.

Bernie Parent with Michele Paiva & Dean Smith

Part Three

Unleash the Wolf

Unleashing the wolf is the culmination of understanding, the foundations of how to find and define your purpose, understanding through examples that I've been able to share in my own life, and now, taking some aspects a little deeper so that you can apply them to your life with verve. You'll also find a worksheet to help guide you through the maze of purpose, and you'll also find online support as well, on my site, www.bernieparent.net, as well as workshops, seminars and more. For now, let's dig a little deeper to help you with details you may not have considered, that will make all the difference in the world in helping you find your purpose and even better, to living your purpose.

Chapter One

Pinpoint Fear

We have discussed purpose, fear, vision, acceptance, people, places and things, a bit of my background and so much more. But let's really apply this to you, because this book isn't about me; it's about you finding your inner wolf, and unleashing it. You have a lot of tools, and I've asked you a lot of introspective questions but we need to delve more deeply now and really decide how you are going to make changes in your life in a methodical way.

I realize you may not be ready. You may have to put this book down and revisit it in a few days, months or even years; however, when you do revisit it, it won't seem as daunting to you, and you'll be able to find that excitement within, anticipate what the future holds and make changes that are action and result oriented.

Let's begin with what holds most people back: Pinpointing your Fears. Let's look at the reality of fears. Fears are a fabrication of your mind. Of course, some fears are valid and some fears are based upon knowledge, but most fears are based upon insecurities rather than tactile instruments or perilous concepts.

Now, don't discount fear. Fear is an emotion; nothing more. And that emotion is there to show us that something needs to be fixed. The fixing may not be *what* you fear but **why** you fear something. Do you fear going forward with a business venture because you are worried what people will say about you? Your fear then is about your dependence upon others' opinions of you, not going forward with a new business venture. Are you fearful of losing money? Your fear is that you won't have enough to live on as you do now, or that your will somehow fall short. Then, what you do is, if that is really your fear, prepare by saving or getting a loan or whatever it is to make that fear vanish. The point is most fears are easily addressed if you pinpoint what they really are based on.

Fear is not only an emotion that can keep us safe, but it is an emotion, like any emotion, that can be crippling. Fear, when abused by our minds, can keep us from achieving dreams. Think of fear as a brick wall. It keeps us from not only getting through to the other side of it, but it keeps us from seeing the benefits of breaking through the wall. However, if you look, you can break the wall down, go around the wall, dig below or rise above it. A brick wall is simply a bunch of blocks of cement and clay; bricks can be broken and taken apart. See the wall that keeps you from achieving your dreams and goals as it is, and then, address it with a vengeance! When stress or fear is coming at you, do you duck or do you look at it head-on? Do you avoid it or tackle it? Do you really know which fears you have or are there so many that you feel like you are in quicksand or cement; just stuck? Fear can help protect you, but if abused by your mind in a way that stops you from living, it can hold you back or even take you backward in your life. Sometimes, I feel that fear is just an easy way to avoid failure. If a person stays at status quo, then they never have to try to find more success or betterment in their life, and that is a great way to avoid perceived failure. However, failure isn't a big deal. I do not know of one successful person who fears failure, and I don't know of one successful person who hasn't experienced quite a bit of failure in life. Have you ever been in a sauna? It's hot and steamy; very hot and steamy. If not, how about a hot shower? At first when you walk in, you feel overwhelmed by the heat, and you may even feel like you can't breathe, but as you allow yourself to relax, you see there is nothing to fear. You can breathe just fine. Fear is the same. At first you want to get away from it but if you sink into it and experience it, it suddenly isn't too big of a deal and you can even find something wonderful in the experience that is freeing. Have you heard the phrase, "if you can't stand the heat, get out of the kitchen?" That's a phrase that pinpoints fear. If it is too much for you to sweat a little and experience a little initial discomfort, you certainly can't be of use to create a recipe and feed yourself much less anyone else. Well, that is fear.

Fear stops you from being able to help yourself or to help others. As I said before, when you have fear, it often shows you just what you need to focus on. Any fear you have now, when it is removed, will only show you more opportunities. Removing a fear is never, ever, going to hold you back. When you overcome a fear you will always feel better afterward. Fear is a tool to help you. If you think of it, fear is like a trusted guide on a journey. Fear is actually the wolf, sniffing through the wild outdoors; finding its way, never knowing what is around the corner. If the wolf just sits and waits, and does not want to explore, it isn't going to go too far. So, fear is just a guide. Would you, if you were out in the wild and lost, turn down a guide? No. You'd see the guide as a teacher or hero. Well, fear is your teacher and your hero. It's there to show you what you need to work on, what you need to address. I cannot possibly know what your specific fears are, but I can tell you that the very things you fear are the very things you need to address. Most times, as I said, fears are just insecurities, or layers of insecurities. We all have them, though not all fears stop us from living a great life. For instance, a fear of being seen as total slob may keep you from leaving your home with your hair unbrushed and your old pajamas on. That is a valid and small fear; it isn't going to keep you back from anything in life. A fear of being burned may help you from playing recklessly with fire. That is a valid fear that keeps you safe. However, a fear of being your own person, or trying something new, or living a dream; these are debilitating fears. Layers of fears come in all shapes and sizes and some are minor, some keep us alive and well, and some are abuses of our mind and debilitating. Facing your fear means to stop judging yourself, and to step back a bit. Take that energy that you give to fear; be the boss of your own life instead of fear bullying you around, and allow that energy to address the fears and then, free of each fear and judgment of yourself, you can experience the phenomenon of your power. This sensation will help you to realize that the unknown is filled with gifts, even more so than what you encounter in your known reality. When you see this, you are more apt to break from the chains that hold you down, and you unleash your inner wolf a little bit more each time you look fear in the eyes.

Bernie Parent with Michele Paiva & Dean Smith

Chapter Two

Cause and Effect

In science, cause is what happens to make something else happen, and effect is the result of that cause. To determine cause and effect, one must always ask, "Why did it happen?" and to determine effect, "What happened?"

In your life, there are a lot of things that happened because the "why" was generated by something or someone else besides you. The effect could have directly happened to you. In life, this will happen often, but the number of times it happens *not* orchestrated by you, is only a variable. You can create your own cause and effect more often than you think. In life, you can live as a result of everything else or you can be the power behind the results. In hockey, there is a net. You try to get the puck into the net. The net is a perimeter. A lot of people can shoot the puck and some get close to the net, a few make it in the net, but most miss the net. The net is there to define the goal. In life also, you put up your own net.

You define your own goals. Some goals make it in the net, some goals are close, while some goals don't make it at all. However, if you don't put up a net, you never can measure how close, or how far, you get from the goal. In order to have a "net" you have to believe in yourself. You have to believe that you can bring cause and effect into your life. If you don't believe in yourself, if you feel your exposure to knowledge, training and behaviors is not worthwhile, if you feel you cannot venture into life and apply these assets, then you won't feel you can create. If you feel you cannot create or "do" then you do not believe in yourself enough. Remember, I had a lot of times where others didn't believe in me but I had to believe in myself. It was not someone else's opinion or perception of me that created cause and effect all the time, it was my own perception. Even when someone else did believe in me, I still had to believe in myself to make cause turn into effect. You can have all the self-help books around you, study with the greatest gurus of all time and go through the motions, but if you don't have certainty in yourself, then you will not go too far.

It's not enough to be somewhat confident or self-assured; you have to have a true, abounding belief in yourself. You will need this so that you can put everything else into action; for without it, it's going to be a very tough journey, more than it needs to be.

To have conviction in yourself is a beautiful thing. Although to be confident and show certainty is not something we can find, it's something we either know or don't know. It's not a halfway thing. If you are "sort of" confident you are not confident. It's all or nothing; the way to get it is to just keep focusing on knowing that you "can" and you "will" be more certain of yourself. There is nothing stopping you from believing in yourself except your own insecurities and thoughts.

Nothing, and I mean nothing, should hinder your dreams. No degree, no personal contacts, no flashy home, clothes or car, is going to get you where you need to be. These items can help, but are completely useless if you can not apply your confidence to every pore of your being.

Think of yourself as a builder. There is everything in front of you to build a home, such as tools and wood. Your confidence is the electricity and energy that makes the tools work, and makes you have strength to move the lumber. Without energy, you just have a heap of stuff. Many people live their lives with a "heap of stuff" around them; opportunities, tools, resources, contacts and more. Very few have the confidence to pool all of their energy at any given moment into putting all of these gifts into action, and creating something, be it a relationship, a career or a life-long goal.

So, if you become your own boss, you are not at the whim of the externals that surround you, but instead are the manager of your own life. You have the authority to create and to bring cause and effect into your own life; you have the power to unleash yourself when you believe in yourself.

Bernie Parent with Michele Paiva & Dean Smith

Chapter Three

Time

We talked about "time" before, remember? But let's take that topic deeper now. Think about this. What possibilities open when you can look fear in the eyes and you feel confident in your ability to control cause and effect? The possibilities change quite a bit from the person who is fearful and sheltered within their own walls and who feels that their life is out of their control. Now, take the more empowered person, the one who is unleashing their inner wolf, and take a look at cause and effect more deeply. When they look at time, it is not a measurement that they worry about; it is simply the space between cause and effect. If you think you have time all figured out, you are mistaken. Even scientists are still trying to figure out the concept of time. We know, as I said before, that time is even perceived differently according to age, and according to the mindset. Think of a time when you really enjoyed what you were doing and time seemed to go so fast, or when you didn't enjoy yourself and time seemed to drag. Now think about when you were a child and summers seemed to last forever. Time is not as easily measured as we think it is. We have mechanical ways to measure time but that doesn't mean it is figured out! So, the concept of time, for the purpose of the wolf, is to simply understand that there is space between cause and effect. What you do with the "space" in your life is up to you. If you choose to sit and watch TV all the time, not to work on bettering yourself, you will find that time isn't very precious. If you instead forge bonding friendships and network with people to create a pack, to learn and evolve, you will find that your time is much more precious. The space between cause and effect is instrumental to your success, because it is a gift of free will. Every time you have "time" on your side or space to fill, you have an opportunity to be free. How you create and shape that freedom is up to you. Here is where purpose and vision really come together. In that space between cause and effect, in our "time" space, we need to spend a certain amount of time (and that depends upon your level of desire and commitment) on our purpose, with all the items that go into purpose (vision, attraction, risk and so on).

When we have that space or what we feel is free time, we often are distracted when we really need to surrender our minds to our purpose more instead of surrendering to our distractions. If we don't focus on purpose, we are focusing on anything BUT our purpose. That isn't going to help us. Now, that does not mean you need give up hobbies, in fact, quite the opposite. Forging an eclectic life filled with diverse interests is quite enriching. However, those interests should all be positive and productive in your life; don't allow anything to get in the way of you and your purpose. If not, your time then is being wasted or in other words, the windows of opportunity could be closing. We all have the same amount of time in terms of how our society measures time; when you hear someone stating that they do not have enough time, what they are really complaining about is their inability to properly focus on their windows of opportunities, or the spaces between cause and effect. It is probable that in at least some ways, they are not at the helm of their own ship; not in

charge of their own cause and effect. They are out of
control and it has little to do with the amount of time
that they have. We all have, in terms of measurement,
the same 24 hours, the same concept of a year, a month,
minutes and seconds. However, what we do with that
measurement of time is the real secret.

Many people have long-term goals, which is fantastic.
However, think about this. If you are more in control of
your own cause and effect, and are more self-motivated
to focus on the space between cause and effect, your
goals naturally are in a shorter gain range. The more
you can actively pursue them, the closer they can
become. The less energy you give to them, the more
they need to be planned at length. The space between
cause and effect directly responds to what you do with
the space between cause and effect.

Here is a very easy example. Think of people who begin
a diet, for instance, on January first. They talk about it
and say how they are going to lose twenty pounds or ten
pounds by summer. They set the date.

Well, what happens between January 1st and June 1st is
the space between cause and effect; it is what you do
with that time, the space between that matters. This is
part of the reason that so many diets, goals, plans,
businesses, relationships and purposes fizzle out. There
has to be a focus on what to do with that time in that
space we have decided and measured; if we don't have
focus, we are out of control.

If you don't focus, you can be a self-professed victim of
being in the wrong place at the wrong time, unlucky, or

without resources. When we are at our darker hours, we tend to make decisions that simply save us rather than raise us.

For instance, to give a more radical example....A man may choose to not work, because he opts for a more leisure lifestyle and lies to others about his situation. He may spend frivolously and be irresponsible. Pretty soon, he has to deal with the ramifications of his life choices, which may include being quite poor and even carry emotional shame and a loss of relationships because of his life choices.

The space between wanting an easier life and the result, which was a failing situation, was his choice all along, but at the end he may consider himself a victim of circumstances. He wasn't a victim at all, he was at the helm of his own boat but he simply was just drifting around, going with the wind and waves rather than having direction.

There is a lot you can be doing right now that you may not be doing to get to the life you wish to live. The spaces of time in your life are not going to change, it is simply your behavior and action that controls what happens in that space. A lot of us waste time; and that is fine if it doesn't get in the way of your life purpose. I am not talking about taking relaxing breaks or spending some time idle; that is a choice. Wasting time is more a waste of a resource, that space you can apply to your happiness.

Think of your life goals and purposes like a kettle of soup. The bigger purpose is the meat. The smaller goals

and desires are the vegetables and everything that helps
you get to desires and purpose is symbolized by the
water, which will become broth.

Now, how you make the soup is you get your purpose
(meat) and put it in the kettle. You cut the vegetables
and add spices (goals and desires) and then, with the
remaining space, you add (resources, tools) water. That
is how you make sure you get everything you need into
the kettle, in there.

If you look at a life perhaps out of control you can
compare it to a soup made sloppily. If you just fill a
kettle with water and start throwing in, haphazardly, the
meat and vegetables, you may notice that the soup spills
over the kettle or you can't fit everything you want into
the kettle. The broth may be too weak even. This is like
life. The space in the kettle is like the space in your life.
You need to keep the meat in that kettle. You need to
keep your purpose in your life. The things you need to
flavor the broth and meat, the vegetables, they need
room in that kettle or it is not going to be the same
soup, or if you don't have the correct blend of goals,
visions and dreams, the purpose will not turn out the
same at all. The remaining space should not be just
"air". It has to be water to turn into broth. If you just
have a life without resources, without a pack, without
tools, without learning, then you just have plain old
water. When you fill the kettle with water, letting it
mingle with the meat and vegetables, then you get a
rich, nourishing broth.

So, if you can visualize, the space in your life is very
much like the space in a kettle for soup; every space

Bernie Parent with Michele Paiva & Dean Smith

within the kettle serves a clear purpose even though
they seem unrelated at times, for the purpose. The cause
and effect are there, and the result is the finished soup
or the purpose lived.

Productive priorities are the actions that bring your time
to be the space that helps you achieve your purpose.
The wolf uses all of the space, the time between his
goals, to further his goals. He even his runs and rests
help him to hone his hunting skills. Make sure your
inner wolf understands the concept of time as it applies
to purpose.

Bernie Parent with Michele Paiva & Dean Smith

Chapter Four

Problem Solving

Although one must have problem solving skills, problem solving should not be your focus unless for whatever reason, problem solving, as a whole, is your purpose. Even then, you can't solve all problems so hear me out on this.

In corporate environments people often talk about "putting out fires". That is another way to say "fixing mistakes". Now, a problem isn't always a mistake, but a mistake is almost always a problem. Mistakes happen when purpose, resources, vision, dedication or simple focus, falters. We think we are being productive when we problem solve, and many of us get caught up in other people's problems, and help them. We, as social beings, and as pack animals, like to feel needed. We enjoy feeling useful. There are even studies that people who volunteer live longer, so helping others is ingrained in our very DNA.

However, when we help others at the sacrifice of ourselves, it is said to be codependent or enabling. That means you are sacrificing far too much and are putting your own sense of self at risk.

What really happens when we problem solve too much, is that we lose focus of purpose and we become emotional and intellectual fire fighters. We run around putting out fires. As soon as we relax, another fire crops up. Remember how we discussed attraction? If we focus

on problem solving, guess what is attracted to us?
Problems!

I love to watch the Three Stooges; you may recall this
was even a part of my relaxation even back in my
hockey playing days. The Three Stooges often were
focused on putting out fires, and they would run around
with a frantic demeanor, and bump into each other and,
in the end, their lack of focus became even worse than
the initial problems that they would try to address!
When you look at a comedy like that, sure you can
laugh, but it isn't so funny when it is you doing the
frantic running around with no focus, is it?

When you focus on problems you think that you can do
the things you desire or need, once you can relax. Well,
that means that the problems are the boss of your life,
controlling you. You have failed then, to take control
over your life. Stop focusing on the problems, and start
focusing on what you can do to live a life that has fewer
problems.

I told you early on, if something isn't working, that
means you have to change it. This is the same for
problems. Now of course, some problems need to be
addressed and we will get into that later, but for now,
realize that a lot of the problems you have probably
were created by you in some way. Sure you may not
have created the exact situation but you on some level,
may have created the foundation to make that situation
too easily a guest in your life; and you can most
certainly escort problems out the door by making
different choices in your life.

Bernie Parent with Michele Paiva & Dean Smith

Have you ever heard the advice that once you ignore something it will go away? Sometimes it is a tantrum or attention given to the negative behavior of an adult that will fizzle out. Think about it.

Problems that are not necessary are the same. Stop focusing on the problems in your life and the problems will have less power; the problematic situations really won't change that much but how you respond will. This change is an exchange in energy. When your energy begins to go in a different direction, it will start to go through a metamorphosis. That change of your energy will go from worry, anger or anxiety to powerful stuff; to a place where you can work on your desires and purpose. Soon the situations that once seemed like a problem will seem minor. If you think back in life, some of the things you felt were problems when you were younger seem minor now. It's because you not only "got through it" but because as you grew and changed focus, you gave that issue less power. People who still harbor issues from when they were younger sometimes are simply holding on and keeping a focus; and if they change it, they will be happier. The biggest secret in problem solving is responsibility. Even if you make a horrible mistake, instead of living in shame or anger, and of course, you are human so you must experience the emotion a short while; you need to get over it! You are a book, turn the page! What happens on the next page? Don't stay on the same page day after day! Be responsible and plan.

One way to address a problem in the now is to ask yourself an honest "Why?"

Bernie Parent with Michele Paiva & Dean Smith

Why did your client drop you?

Why did something take too long?

Why did you gain weight?

Why did you pick up a cigarette after not smoking for three months?

Why did you let your in-laws get to you again?

Do you see the trend here? You need to be honest. In each of these questions, you need to delve deeper.

Let's look at "Why did your client drop you?"

Is it that they just didn't like you? Were you not working with them properly? Were you hard to work with? Did you show respect or a lack of respect? Did you take pride in your work? Were you ethical?

How about the cigarette problem?

Did you suddenly just have a craving that was overwhelming? What brought on that craving? Can you stop after that one pitfall? What did that caving in mean to you? Did having that cigarette bring up feelings of failure rooted deeply within you? What was it that started you on the addiction?

Problems are opportunities to change and grow, and yes, they are problems also. For the most part, you can overcome your problems.

How many problems in your life are your own
problems? How many do you take on to make other's
lives easier? How can you decrease problems in your
life? How can you best apply problem-solving skills to
turn the page in your book of life?

A wolf doesn't dwell; a wolf solves a problem or
accepts the reality in front of him and works with it. A
wolf is a member of the pack and responsible for
himself and himself only; he is not responsible for the
pack. You should take clues from the wolf, and
remember that you can address a problem, work with it
and be responsible only for your own issues. Don't own
problems, they are just distractions meant to keep you
from your purpose.

Bernie Parent with Michele Paiva & Dean Smith

Bernie Parent with Michele Paiva & Dean Smith

Chapter Five

Money

This is going to be a short chapter and one you may not like at first. Money, the coins and paper you exchange for clothes, cars and real estate, is just a symbol. The value of the money, the symbols; are simply a consciousness of a collective agreement. If the paper dollar in your hand is only said to be worth thirteen cents, that is all it is worth. If it is worth what is known as a dollar and fifty cents, that is what it is worth. The actual money you hold or that is in your bank account actually changes often.

We see this with Wall Street; we see this in real estate. The worth of money fluctuates. What matters is your attitude about money more than anything else. If you see money the ultimate value, as something to chase, or feel you will never be "wealthy" chances are you will live paycheck to paycheck at best. If you see money as simply one of many forms of value in your life, and are a more generous person, chances are money will flow to you more readily.

The value of money is simply energy. If you don't recognize that money is simply a conscious energy, you may find that it slips away from you all too often.

Bernie Parent with Michele Paiva & Dean Smith

If you harbor anger, envy or resentment toward those who are wealthy, not only are you putting energy into a negative focus but you are simply focusing on someone else and not yourself. If you focus on what you do not have, guess what; you seem to make a self-fulfilling prophecy and do not have much. Meanwhile, the reality may be different. You could feel like you are poor, be miserable and jealous and actually have financial wealth. Did you ever notice that money actually never makes anyone happy who has had it a long time, and that people who are poor are not always unhappy even if they have been poor a long time? It's because money doesn't create your life energy or happiness; it is how you respond that creates your happiness. In your life there will be people who will envy you, and you may not even know it.

There will be people who envy you, gossip about you and wish you unwell. Everything has energy, so their negative energy could bring you down if you do not focus on your positive energy. Think about it. Being happy protects you from negative people. If you are already feeling down, a negative word can make you feel worse. If you feel good about yourself and your situation, then a negative word will be seen as just that; an unhappy person using you as their scapegoat and target.

That won't bother you too much because, well, your value isn't in money, what you are worth on society's paper trail in the bank or someone else's opinion of "worth" of you.

Bernie Parent with Michele Paiva & Dean Smith

Worth is a wide focus, yet it is often under-discussed.
That being said, in our society, we do often need some
type of financial comfort zone to not live in total
poverty; and many of us focus on just having enough,
and guess what.

Many of us have just enough. If you want your purpose
you need to let go of focusing on the value of yourself
and what you own, and know that it is enough.
Focusing on what you don't have is not going to help
your purpose.

The wolf doesn't need to control all of nature or own all
of nature to be happy; the wolf is happy with what they
have, and they always seem to have enough.

It's always better to have enough and be able to share,
and to be happy, then to feel like you don't have enough
and be unhappy and unwilling to share.

Bernie Parent with Michele Paiva & Dean Smith

Bernie Parent with Michele Paiva & Dean Smith

Chapter Six

Be Yourself

This sounds like a given. Think about it. How many of
you, in your work, with certain neighbors or friends or
even in different clubs, put on small facades? We don't
need to wear every emotion or thought on our sleeves of
course, but in whole, we should be happy in our own
skin. You can't be yourself only 50% of the time or 60%
of the time, you need to be yourself 100% of the time.
The reason is that to arrive at your purpose you need to
be authentic to yourself and not juggle images of who
you are, unless you are an actor. Being authentic is a
character virtue, one that is welcomed in sales to self-
employment, or lovers' relationships to friendships.
Peers, friends and family all should respect your
authentic self and those who do not, well, you probably
do not need them in your life. You have heard about the
warning of a wolf in sheep's clothing. There is nothing
wrong with a wolf, but a wolf pretending to be
something he isn't, well, that is misleading and
unethical. If you have a hunger to create and live your
purpose, then you need to be happy in your own skin,
not in anybody else's skin. We are all unique, and if
you are afraid of your individuality, then you are not
comfortable with yourself and you are simply a wolf in
sheep's clothing. Sheep run in large herds and are easily
led. We hear sheep being compared to the mass of
people who may blinded by false statements or swayed
by propaganda. Docile and dumb are the images of a
herd of sheep when spoken about in that manner. So,
are you a sheep or a wolf? If you want to lead and not

be led, you need to be a leader. You can run in a pack, but you can not just follow the herd. In order to lead, in order to carve your way, you need to be your own person, and you can not be your own person if you can't be true to yourself. If you can't be true to yourself, how can you arrive at a "your" purpose if it is not "you" arriving? Many people refuse to be themselves because they have shame. They may have skeletons in their closet or have situations that they are not proud of. Maybe you are one of these people. Do you have episodes in your life that you are ashamed of, or mistakes that you regret? It is fine to not be proud of every downfall, but if you can turn your mistakes or issues into lessons you have learned from, guess what. You have the opportunity to become an inspiration to others. I talked about how my drinking was a problem, and I could easily be someone who holds shame in that. However, I don't hold shame. Think about it. I learned from my situations, mistakes and obstacles surrounding drinking. I can be inspiring to someone who may be in the throes of alcoholism right now. Mistakes are opportunities to inspire others. Start being proud of every aspect of who you are. Whenever the voice of self-doubt sneaks into your mind, stop and think about what I am telling you here. How can you turn that negative thought and energy into a way to celebrate where you are now, and how can you inspire others?

Diamonds are just coal. A wolf is a living creature. You are unique. Unleash yourself and allow yourself to embrace who you are so that others can learn from you, so that you can be proud of who you are, and so your purpose is more streamlined and authentic.

Bernie Parent with Michele Paiva & Dean Smith

Chapter Seven

Infinite Possibilities

I've said before that often people begin to find that they have more than one purpose, more than one vision; many goals and dreams. If this has not happened to you yet, do not worry. It may not, but more than likely, it will. When it does happen, you may be so programmed by society to whittle down your "focus" and just concentrate on one thing. I do not agree. Infinite possibilities are a beautiful thing. When you have a purpose, you have an intimate feeling connected to an idea or focus. You feel intimate about your goals. You become one with your purpose. When you think about your purpose, you tend to spend time daydreaming about the "what if" possibilities, and when you are in the flow of your purpose, you are exceptionally happy. Your purpose has meaning.

When you have meaning this powerful, good things happen. The universe brings you more. Your pack becomes larger. Your confidence soars, your ability to empathize with others increases. You often feel like you've grown spiritually and intellectually by leaps and bounds. When you have this passion, when you have an honor of time, of that space between cause and effect, when you are authentic, when you see value in yourself, and when you focus on only real and valid problems, you suddenly have an enhanced integrity. It is not the integrity that you show the world, it is instead your ability to tie into the world, to tie into the universe.

Bernie Parent with Michele Paiva & Dean Smith

Your opportunities expand. You pick and choose which
opportunities to take, based upon your authentic self,
rather than chase opportunities. When we discuss pride
in our purpose, sometimes that word, "pride" turns
people off. There is no shame in having meaning in
your life. There is no shame in *feeling* meaning in your
life. If you dislike the word "proud" then you are not
comfortable with pride. To not be able to feel and
express meaning and pride, strongly curtails your
possibilities. When we have a purpose, our pack
increases, and as our pack increases we learn more. We
become better people based upon the people we allow
into our lives. We can help others and that feels good.
Our world opens up more and more, and suddenly the
universe is more within us. It doesn't matter what your
purpose is; you will begin to meet many interesting
people. Think about it. The people you meet are
possibly working toward their purpose, and focusing on
their authentic self, and also looking to face fear, and be
a member of the pack. The possibilities are endless.
You may get involved in fundraisers, educational fairs,
scientific studies and much more; all avenues that
greatly help others and bring you rich experiences even
if they are not in your direct purpose. Then, you get
involved in these opportunities and you meet more
people, with even more opportunities. The world is
there for you to experience, and the experiences are
within you to unleash. Do not ever let anyone critique
you to the point of squashing your dreams, your
opportunities or putting a lid on how much you can
experience. I, and now you, know that possibilities for
you are infinite. No wolf is told that he can't wander. He
just does, and he experiences. Do not be put on a leash,
ever.

Bernie Parent with Michele Paiva & Dean Smith

Chapter Eight

Potential

Similar to possibilities is potential. This is another area that externally you may be told that you do not have the "potential" to reach your purpose, goals or dreams. Remember, I was told that I should not even get involved in ice hockey, in short, because I didn't have the "potential" according to other people.

Potential is really nothing more than stored energy. In some terms it can be called "promise". If someone shows "promise" at being a piano player, they are encouraged, but if they do not show "promise" then they are sometimes not only *not* encouraged but discouraged. Realize that promise and potential are all external observations. Think about that. It has very little to do with how the individual feels, or what he really has within him.

Even we, as individuals, do not know our true potential. We cannot possibly comprehend what our capacity is, as it is impossible to measure. Because of this, my feeling is that we need to not put a lid on our potential. I don't want you to allow anyone to tell you what your potential is. Remember this pep talk that I'm giving you if they try. You don't have to debate with them, just ignore them and do your own thing. People can have many jobs, interests and gifts. Even if you have done great things in your life according to others and even if you feel you have; if you want to do more, then do it!

Bernie Parent with Michele Paiva & Dean Smith

Let me give you an example. Let's say you are a
neurosurgeon. Maybe you developed a breakthrough in
science. Maybe you have fulfilled dreams of marrying a
true love and have children and a beautiful home.
However, maybe you also feel you want to be a concert
pianist. People may wonder why you are not already
happy with all that you have. You may be told that you
should focus on what you know and externally, feel
guilt for wanting to pursue a goal or purpose.

Don't let anyone hold you back. Many successful
people are not seeking money or power when they seek
purpose. You will find that the more you reach goals
and purpose the more that the experience of the purpose
is enough for you; even though many other benefits do
follow. Potential is up to you. If you don't live up to the
potential of yourself as you see it, you are missing out
on your birthright. Someone holding you back or down
is essentially enslaving you. Do not allow this.

You can live their way, according to their rules, like
you are a dog, leashed and subservient to their whims,
or you can be a wolf, who lives life to the fullest and is
strong and filled with endurance.

We have options; we can be in a drab existence with an
undeveloped life, or we can be exhilarated in our lives,
possessing a power within and a capable mindset with
which we can experience a life of many potentials.

It's up to you; are you the lacking dog, unable to reach
potential, living for another's joy or, are you the wolf,
who has the aptitude for reaching his potential with a
little sweat and determination?

Bernie Parent with Michele Paiva & Dean Smith

Chapter Nine

Cultivate a Life

Many people just survive, or just barely thrive. It is amazing to me the amount of people who simply do not cultivate their own lives.

Your life is like a garden. You can't just plant it and walk away and expect great things. Sure you may get something out of it but in order to grab that red tomato, you may have to rummage through weeds, ransack past bugs, maybe even get bit or stung a few times, get your feet muddy and end up finding that most of the crop is spoiled or rotting already.

Your life untended is just like this. If you don't cultivate it, it can get pretty murky. You don't notice it happening, just like the garden tends to look weed-heavy overnight.

The reason you need to cultivate a life is that you have to enjoy your life, even when it gets a little trying.

Think about this. If you don't cultivate a life, you won't be curious about the next day. You won't anticipate anything much less good things. Good things come if you anticipate them. Without cultivating a life filled with good people (your pack), you won't have anyone to talk to; to discuss your life with. Failure to thrive is entropy.

Bernie Parent with Michele Paiva & Dean Smith

When you have nothing to do, when you haven't cultivated and you do not focus on cultivating, then your mind just goes to mush. You fall into predicable routines and those bad habits that we learned from generations ago. We only find ourselves focusing or concentrating if we "have" to like when we drive or maybe cook. Other times, our mind wanders with no direction and external junk becomes all we have to focus on. We lose our purpose and we hardly can think about goals because we haven't even cultivated a life much less used our gift of life as a springboard to purpose.

You can tell people who are not in a cultivated life; perhaps even you will find this painfully familiar when I start to mention the signs. Some signs of a non-cultivated life are boredom, watching a lot of television, unpleasant thoughts enter the mind, rehashing of regrets and mistakes, not letting go of the past, depression can surface. A zest for life is simply not there even though you may want to have a passion for life.

Ways to cultivate a life are simple but take practice; you have to really commit. If you don't cultivate a life, you will have a very hard time doing anything else I talked about, so this is a foundation item also, like most of this part of the book. Every morning I want you to have a goal. The goal doesn't have to be about your purpose at all. Just have a goal that you are going to look forward to. Do not beat yourself up if you do not reach that goal. Just be happy to *have* the goal! Think about the artist who embraces life. He wakes up out of bed, filled with the possibility of the day. He has the goal of painting. He may be stuck and not be able to paint that day

because he may not feel inspiration, but he doesn't let
that get him down. He still woke up with the goal and
he'll wake up with a goal the next day and the next day.

Creative people tend to have a bit of an easier time
embracing the daily goals, but you do not have to be
creative to do this. Simply commit to having a goal each
morning to look forward to. That goal need not be
earth-shattering, just meaningful. The goal can be as
simple as calling a different friend daily to ask how they
are. The goal can be to start a project or work on a
project that you enjoy. The goal can be to wear a
favorite cologne each day even if you will be by
yourself. The goals need not be big, just something to
look forward to.

Trivial or not the act of enjoyable goal setting is going
to teach you to cultivate a life.

As you learn to set goals, start to learn to master
something.

It can be minor. Master cleaning the kitchen table every
day. Master making the bed so that it looks like a
magazine cover. Master an instrument or begin
organizing a business if that is what you enjoy. It does
not matter what you do, as soon as you learn to enjoy
mastering skills, you will want to do more. Mastering
even small skills is enjoyable.

The more you enjoy mastering skills, the more skills
you will start to acquire. The more skills you acquire
the more you enjoy goal setting.

Bernie Parent with Michele Paiva & Dean Smith

Soon you will be able to add enjoyable goals, and mastering them also will be enjoyable; and soon you won't even think about it but you will wake up more refreshed, looking forward to a day filled with meaning. You will have learned to cultivate your life.

A wolf is good at hunting and surviving. He does more than the bare minimum. He lives his life to his fullest. He cultivates his life.

His journey through risk and fear is just as much about enjoying his life as it is surviving.

Bernie Parent with Michele Paiva & Dean Smith

Chapter Ten

Your Turn

In the development of this book, I had many meetings with people from many paths of my life. Because I live, not just talk about the "pack", I bounced around ideas for the name of the book, subtitles and what the end product should look like.

I decided that the book needed to be a book unlike any other, where the reader can not only have text to read and a workbook available (online) but a way to customize the book. After all, the entire premise of this book is that we all are unique with different purposes.

So, in this chapter, it's going to be more about you. I don't want you to just read the book and put it down; I want you to take action. Remember, action will get you to your purpose.

You may want to use a different paper to write your answers down so that you can revisit this as your purpose changes or evolves, as it probably will. Take a moment to skim through the book, perhaps highlight areas of interest that resound to you, and then come back here and begin answering some questions. For further training and coaching, please visit my website, www.bernieparent.net, for downloads and much more.

The title of this book; did it resound to you and how did it make you feel initially?

After you read the book, what was your take on the title of the book, and how does it resound to you right now?

If you had to reach into your heart or spirit, what would you say your purpose is? Are there several? What are they?

In a perfect world, what would you be doing right now?

If you had the infinite possibility, what would your life look like down to the home you live in to the job you do (if you work) and where you travel?

Now, let's look at life right now. What is your life like?

Is your life near what you'd like it to be? How much has to change?

Bernie Parent with Michele Paiva & Dean Smith

What fears do you have about change or, simply, what are your fears?

Explore your vision... how do you envision at least one goal or purpose? What do you see?

How will you overcome your fears to make this vision a reality?

When have you turned your back on safety and felt empowered by that action?

Who are people, place and things in your life that have been a help to you?

With people, places and things that have not been as helpful, what have you learned to be an inspiration to yourself and perhaps to others?

Bernie Parent with Michele Paiva & Dean Smith

Develop at least three small goals to implement each morning to cultivate a life that is more fruitful.

Name three tasks you are going to work on and master, even if minor, to help cultivate a life that is more enjoyable.

When did you have a time in your life (if at all) that you felt someone held you back from your potential?

Based upon your new information in this book, would you now react differently and if not, how will you make changes to react differently to someone holding you back from your potential?

How will you slowly shed layers of lack of authenticity, so that you can be yourself more and more (if this is an issue)?

Bernie Parent with Michele Paiva & Dean Smith

I want to hear about your journey! I want to hear how you unleash your inner wolf! Visit my site, fill out the form and keep me updated at www.bernieparent.net

Be sure to also visit the Philadelphia Flyers at

www.philadelphiaflyers.com

Do you have a book idea or would like to contact the publisher and author? Please contact

www.michelepaiva.com, Balletsa Inc.

Dean Smith

Manager to Bernie Parent

For all inquiries regarding Bernie Parent, or concerning this book including but not limited to speaking and media, with Parent or Paiva, Contact Dean Smith, Manager

856 988 0001

ds@bernieparent.net

Bernie Parent with Michele Paiva & Dean Smith

Bernie Parent with Michele Paiva & Dean Smith

About Michele Paiva & Dean Smith

Michele Paiva: With over twenty years working in media, Paiva is a former print journalist, broadcast reporter & anchor as well as television choreographer. With a strong background in the arts and yoga, she owned a studio for 18 years She has been a member of the American Psychological Association and American Bar Association. The author of eleven books, and the founder of Balletsa Publishing, she resides in Chester County. Find out more at www.michelepaiva.com

Dean Smith: A successful entrepreneur and businessman with expertise in a multitude of areas. His friendship with Parent, which preceded managing Parent, began with a passion for hunting and fishing, and the focus on family values etched the friendship in stone. With friendship first, Smith has helped Parent blaze a path of prosperity with shared ethics and sound fundamentals of doing the right thing. He can be reached at ds@bernieparent.net   www.bernieparent.net

Notes

Bernie Parent with Michele Paiva & Dean Smith

Bernie Parent with Michele Paiva & Dean Smith